Effecting Change in Psychotherapy

Effecting Change in Psychotherapy

Stephen A. Appelbaum

NEW YORK   **Jason Aronson**   LONDON

Publishers of the following journals and books have given permission to adapt and reprint here material originally published by them: Chapter 1 *Bulletin of the Menninger Clinic* (1978) 42(3):239–251, Chapter 2 *Perspectives* (1977) 7(4): 16–17, Chapter 3 *International Journal of Psychoanalytic Psychotherapy* (1975) 4:272–302, Chapter 5 *International Journal of Psychoanalytic Psychotherapy* (1975) 4:426–436 and *Psychiatry* (1967) 30:276–282, Chapter 6 *Journal of the American Psychoanalytic Association* (1966) 14:462–477, Chapter 7 *International Journal of Psycho-Analysis* (1973) 54:35–46, Chapter 8 Smith, S., ed. (1978). *The Human Mind Revisited: Essays in Honor of Karl A. Menninger*. New York: International University Press, Chapter 10 *The Handbook of Gestalt Therapy* (1976). New York: Jason Aronson and Appelbaum, S. A. (1979). *Out in Inner Space — A Psychoanalyst Explores the New Therapies*. New York: Doubleday/Anchor, and Chapter 11 *Inter-American Journal of Psychology* (1975) 1–2:213–220.

To
Brooks Carol Appelbaum
and
Eric Nicholas Appelbaum

Contents

Acknowledgments

One of the advantages of my 21 years at the Menninger Foundation was to be exposed to the ideas and editing of many top-flight colleagues. Among those colleagues who have contributed to this book in these ways are Drs. Ann Halsell Appelbaum, who creatively edited both this and many other of my writings, Martin Mayman, Ishak Ramzy, Sydney Smith, Herbert J. Schlesinger, and Philip S. Holzman, who also wrote with me the first section of Chapter 5. I greatly appreciate the help of all of them.

Part I

Elements in the Process of Change

Almost yesterday, as the history of ideas is measured, people did not discuss their neuroses on television, information about new therapies was not delivered with the morning newspaper, and cocktail party conversation consisted of topics other than what one's analyst had said. In that context it was unremarkable that I, as a new student of psychotherapy,* was asked, in a voice full of incredulity, "How do people change just through talking?" Not feeling the support of wide cultural acceptance and unsure just how change is effected, I became defensive. Words like "insight," "ego," and "transference" rushed to my mind, though I realized that I could not

*Throughout the book, unless otherwise specified, "psychotherapy" refers to psychoanalytic psychotherapy, which is a process informed by the principles underlying psychoanalysis. The techniques used in that process may be those customarily referred to as psychoanalysis or variations customarily referred to as "psychoanalytic" or "dynamic" psychotherapy.

use these words to make clear to my innocent interrogator how people change. Indeed, what these words precisely referred to, and how whatever they referred to was related to change in psychotherapy, was not entirely clear to me, either. For a long time I pursued the question of how change occurs in psychotherapy, and I still do. In recent years that pursuit has been enhanced by my studies of the so-called new therapies, particularly those of the "human potential" movement. (The results of those studies are recorded in my *Out in Inner Space — A Psychoanalyst Explores the New Therapies* [1979b]). I have become increasingly aware of the healing context of all psychotherapies: the therapeutic influences that can act as agents of beneficial change in any procedure that purports to be therapeutic. Both my old interrogator's incredulity and my defensiveness could have been avoided if we had viewed psychotherapy less as a new, discrete invention and more as a refinement — great as that refinement is — of centuries of healing procedures.

All through history people have apparently benefited from talking to one another, sometimes combined with sharing activities specific to a particular calling and time. They seem to have been helped by talk over backyard fences and over teacups, with medicine men and witch doctors, with priests and gurus, and with healers who appear to do no more than lay on their hands. Presumably such efforts would not have continued and would not have become institutionalized over the centuries had they not somehow been helpful.

My interrogator of years back, long since having become a citizen-intellectual, would probably not repeat his question today. More is the pity; it was and still is a good question. The surge in acceptance of psychotherapy in the last three decades has not been fully matched by an accumulation of knowledge of how psychotherapy "works." Often psychotherapists and researchers fail to specify even what "works" refers to, for what people, under what circumstances, with what therapists, to what ends, and how whatever happens comes about. Nonetheless, if asked the question now, I would be more confident that psychotherapy indeed does work, and I would be able to clarify better those factors that explain how people change "just by talking."

One category of factors responsible for the change in psychotherapy is that of the techniques employed by the therapist, often for a particular kind of therapy (for example, insight). Another category is of those factors that function silently, that may not be chosen intentionally by the therapist, and that may not be specific to any one therapy (for example, having a helper with one's life). Some factors may be used deliberately or may be silent and involuntary (for example, behavior modification, the use of the interpersonal relationship, and suggestion). Elements from all categories are almost invariably commingled in any intervention.

Another, somewhat more discrete category contains those qualities in the psychotherapist that either encourage or inhibit change in psychotherapy. Such qualities include not only the obvious ones learned in the formal training to become a psychotherapist, such as a knowledge of theory and technique, but also personal qualities such as those that inspire confidence or supply a model. I have named one of these personal qualities "evocativeness," a term that refers to the many ways in which psychotherapy can be made vivid and memorable.

Chapter 1 offers an overview of many of these factors that encourage change in psychotherapy, of which several will be explored in greater detail in the succeeding chapters.

1

Pathways to Change in Psychoanalytic Therapy

Talking

One reason that we are surprised that change can come about "just through talking" is that many people have become accustomed to believing that any sort of progress is dependent upon an ever proliferating array of gadgetry interposed between an ill person and a healer. From the stethoscope between the physician's ear and the patient's chest to the angiogram and the electrocardiogram, scientific and technological advances have quite understandably created a mixture of gratitude, awe, and faith in all of us. It is no wonder then that something so simple and direct as mere talking seems regressive, an abandonment of hard-won scientific gains. Psychotherapy, however, is not mere "talk"; indeed, talking is more than "just talk," for the step from thoughts in the mind to the spoken word is complex and often decisive.

Words are structures, and when thoughts form a structure they become more clear. Thus, many people report that they did not know what they thought until they heard themselves say it. Words also are public. By translating thoughts into words a person commits himself and lets others know what he thinks and where he stands. With such a public commitment he creates dimensions in which to function, boundaries beyond which to operate, and an external reality. Furthermore, words as percepts are different from thoughts as percepts. Thoughts from the inside transferred to words on the outside are new phenomena and offer new opportunities for understanding. Finally, words are a means of establishing and maintaining interpersonal contact. Such verbal contact has its inception in the reciprocal sounds between mother and child, the verbal equivalent of touch. The act, then, of talking may sometimes be more valuable than whatever words may be uttered: What psychotherapist — indeed, what good friend — has never heard the heartfelt, "It was so good just talking to you"?

Insight

True to Freud's seminal observation that he could help a patient get rid of a symptom by discovering a prior event that gave meaning to the symptom, change in psychoanalysis is chiefly identified with understanding, learning the underlying meanings of thoughts and behaviors, and making the unconscious conscious through insight.

By now there should be no doubt that one can gather data that will allow the construction of a pattern of meaning according to the clinical theory of psychoanalysis. Also, by now there should be no doubt that in response to following the rules for ascertaining these data, predictable behaviors will occur: for example, free association will lead to connected thoughts; patients will resist the process of self-discovery. When all is well — the right patient with the right analyst in the right supporting environment — patterns of development will inevitably occur, for example, from dependence to independence, from regression to progression, and from unrealistic ideas (especially about the analyst) to more realistic ones. This process is clearly and unequivocally moved along by felicitous interpretations by the analyst and by meanings cooperatively derived by patient and analyst.

In apparent response to such discoveries, what the patient talks about, and his mood, behavior, and experience of life outside the analytic hours tend to change for the better. Because of

such change, the temptation is to assume a one-to-one correspondence between correct insight and therapeutic change. In so
doing, however, one overlooks the many other possible reasons
for change that have participated, intentionally or unintentionally, in the process of pursuing insight as well as in the overall
process of behavioral change. One also may have elided such
issues as whether change occurs through achieving insight or
whether insight comes about through achieving change, and
other aspects of the relationship between knowledge of the
unconscious life and how the conscious life is lived. By assuming too much too soon about the power of insight, one may fail
to check systematically, for example, what the patient understands as compared to what the psychotherapist understands.
(Most psychotherapists have noticed how often patients remember previous hours differently from the way the analyst remem-
bers them and how hard it is to believe what patients report
about any previous therapies they have had.) Finally, how durable is change brought about by insight, and is such durability
related to other therapeutic factors as well? To many psychotherapists, insight is a thing of beauty and a joy forever. Its
power and dramatic appeal should not, however, lead to its
idealization, at the cost of insufficiently studying insight itself
and of overlooking and underexploiting other means of change.
These issues are discussed in detail in Chapter 3.

Corrective Emotional Experience

For many psychotherapists, corrective emotional experience is associated with Franz Alexander and then dismissed.
Alexander's special use of corrective emotional experience is not
identical with the general process. Generally, corrective emotional experience refers to the nonoccurrence of events that the
patient assumes will occur. As a consequence of this nonoccurrence, he learns that his fantasies need not come true. Alexander
(1946) recommended that the therapist self-consciously dramatize
roles from the patient's repertoire of fantasy figures. But Alexander's procedure is not necessary for the corrective emotional

experiences to occur. Indeed, if the psychotherapist maintains his neutral, nonjudgmental stance, corrective emotional experiences cannot be prevented.

Parenthetically, the very phrase, "corrective emotional experience," is something of a misnomer. It is true that most psychoanalytic learning takes place best when things matter emotionally. But in a corrective emotional experience, ideas and fantasies are corrected as much as are emotional reactions. The phrase could just as well be "corrective ideational experience." But whatever the phrase, patients report that the change in them came about because what they had expected to happen did not happen; for example, the psychotherapist did not reject them despite their acknowledging what they thought were dirty wishes or did not leave them no matter how obstreperous, boring, or, for that matter, how healthfully they behaved.

Interpersonal Relationship

The term "interpersonal relationship" is another rubbery phrase that has led to much misunderstanding and unnecessary heat. Some psychotherapists understand the phrase to refer to a relationship in opposition to an intrapsychic one, a transpersonal transaction more akin to social psychology than to psychotherapy. Indeed, it sometimes has such a meaning and is used to draw a boundary between psychoanalytics and other schools of therapy or professions. But this polarizing of insight versus interpersonal relationship factors in change can lead to an underemphasis of those interpersonal factors that take place even in the most psychoanalytic of therapies. To believe that they do not would be to subscribe to the image that many critics of psychoanalytic therapy have of the psychotherapist as an unfeeling, calculating machine. Such an image would belie the psychoanalytic values inherent in identification and the benevolent modification of both the superego and the internalization of a cooperative, understanding partner for self-analysis and guidance

The concept of the "real" nontransference relationship is one expression of the understanding of interpersonal relationships in psychoanalytic change. Another is the largely British object-relations point of view that psychoanalysis provides a second chance for the patient to grow in a new and improved nurturing environment. The growth-producing qualities of such an environment are said to be more important than the interpretations and understanding that take place in it. A similar emphasis was set forth in American psychoanalysis by Harry Stack Sullivan, Frieda Fromm-Reichman, and Otto Will, among others. A major finding of the Psychotherapy Research Project of the Menninger Foundation was that those patients who had developed the most insight did the best of all. Yet there was another group of patients who, in the absence of much insight and conflict resolution, achieved what was called in the project "structural change," despite the project's conventional assumption that structural change could come about only through conflict resolution (Appelbaum 1977a). One explanation of such a change was that the patients had benefited primarily from the interpersonal relationship with their therapist (Horwitz 1974). A new interpersonal context enabled the patient to resume the arrested development that had led to his symptoms.

Overcoming Apartness

One part of the interpersonal relationship as a pathway to change, but deserving notice in its own right, is the difference between feeling alone, so often a distinguishing characteristic of neurosis, as compared to having somebody to turn to. Freud described a neurotic as someone who is unable to establish membership in a group. The neurotic is solipsistic, he relates himself to himself, and he interacts with his idiosyncratic population of internal images. In this sense, every neurosis is narcissistic, and every neurotic is alone. How much is the distress of neurotic life due to this self-imposed loneliness? How much desperation and pessimism are caused by a lonely struggle with

ghosts? This state of affairs changes immediately when the
patient is accepted for treatment, though patients vary greatly
in the degree to which they accept the interpersonal reality that
we call a therapeutic alliance. That "somebody up there loves
me," or might love me, probably is significant in bringing about
a honeymoon at the beginning of some psychotherapies. As
reality becomes transference and transference becomes transference neurosis, this honeymoon ends. The patient's solitary
preoccupation with fantasy figures continues, but now it is in
relation to a real person. Yet with a patient well selected for
psychotherapy, there always is in such a relationship the
recognition of the real person, the real helper. As with many
teenagers and their parents, and many husbands and wives, the
participants may act as if there were no satisfying connections
between them, no transactions unmarked by idiosyncratic con-
cerns from elsewhere. But at some level of awareness, they
know that they are benevolently attached to one another. When
all goes well and the patient surmounts his difficulties, he does
so partly as a function of the guiding relationship with the
psychotherapist, just as some students learn out of love for their
teachers. Independent of the content of the sessions, this
primordial image of a helper — someone for whom and with whom
to live and someone with whom to work out one's difficulties —
reaches outward and makes workable what otherwise might be
the circular, festering conundrum of neurosis.

Emotional Release

In the beginnings of psychoanalysis, along with the discovery of ideas, was the catharsis of emotion. The contribution to
change of emotional outpouring has survived in psychotherapy,
but usually in the context of suffusing the discovery of meaning
and the reconstruction of events with emotions. That such emotions give ideas and memories an intrapsychic importance
increases their influence and usefulness. In recent years, Janov

(1970) and others demonstrated the great intensity of emotion that can be elicited when releasing emotion is taken as the major task of therapy. In so doing, Janov implicitly raised the issue for psychoanalytic psychotherapy as to how much emotion is enough emotion. He widened the range so that we now see that in psychoanalysis we ordinarily work with only a small part of that range. Whatever the relative contribution of emotion to change proves to be, in calling attention to the possibilities of change through intense emotional expression, Janov refurbished for some of us the recognition that affect ought to be credited explicitly and studied imaginatively.

Suggestion

The word "suggestion" has several meanings. As most commonly used it means to offer an idea, that is, to make a suggestion. It can also refer to forcing one's ideas on another as in brainwashing and thought control. Somewhere between making a suggestion and forcing an idea is the explicit influencing of the patient by supporting a suggestion with the authority engendered by the transference.

In all of these uses of the word "suggestion," one person does something to another, the difference between them dependent only on the amount of force applied. Many people experience this mode of extending help as unsavory; others object to its being nonanalytic, usually meaning noninterpretive. So, to many psychotherapists, suggestion is at best a base form of the copper of psychotherapy and at worst, manipulation. But there is another kind of suggestion, one that does not involve this subject-object mode, one in which no one does anything to anyone else. That is the suggestion, alternatively named "placebo," which silently functions in all therapeutic transactions in which the need to believe and to benefit is strong. Take, for example, the state of mind and feeling of a person pacing around in neurotic circles, knowing he has nowhere to go except where he has unsuccessfully been before, and compare it with the state of mind and feeling of a person in psychotherapy, where with the help of another he is offered the hope of breaking out of his neurotic cage. The patient's attention has somewhere new to go, and his energy has somewhere else to expend itself. He has made a break with the past simply by undertaking therapy, and he backs up his intention to bring about change with the expenditure of time, effort, and money. He thereby produces in himself an expectation and impetus toward change, an autosuggestion. He is aided in this effort by the implicit suggestion that he is to be helped, as conveyed to him by the cultural sanctions that support the offering to him of psychotherapy. By such sanctions, his peers and his social family proffer their like-minded expectation that he is to benefit. That suggestion contributes to change in psychotherapy is, from one point of view, unsettling. Perhaps the patient reports change only because he expects that of himself, or perhaps he behaves differently only because he expects to behave differently; in both instances change would be tied to the treatment and might give way when the treatment is over. But suggestion may also contribute to the analytic process by helping the patient overcome resistances and accept meaning, and by tiding the patient over difficult times. By suggestion the therapist is given the benefit of the doubt so the work can continue. In this sense, suggestion can be considered as mutative and thus deserving study and respect. Copper, too, has important uses.

Coherence and Mastery

As can be seen from some altered states of consciousness, especially dreams, the unconscious mind is chaotic. The psychoanalytic objectives of making the unconscious conscious, of bringing impulses under the sway of the ego, and of shifting from the primary to the secondary process are intended, by definition, to create secondary-process order. When one considers that the patient's experience is often one of confusion, dismay, and a loss of moorings, then it follows that whatever brings about a sense of stability contributes to beneficial change. One way such stability can come about is through a compulsive regime — for example, anchoring the week with psychotherapeutic appointments and the continued opportunity for self-analysis. As Glover (1931) pointed out, even an inexact interpretation has beneficial effects in that it gives the patient something to focus on, thereby helping him bind anxiety, a sort of internal compulsive regime. Another way of creating order is by learning a coherent story of oneself, an encompassing framework that unites seemingly separate events into logical sequences and patterns. Equipped with such coherence, the patient becomes confident that whatever occurs in his life can, in principle, be understood within the framework of his analytic understanding. He knows now that he is less likely to be taken by surprise, to be mystified at what he or others do, think, or feel, and that he has a backlog of information on which to base decisions. With all of these contributing to a sense of mastery, he is no longer subject to what Frank (1974) called "demoralization."

Order through understanding is not necessarily dependent on the accuracy of explanation. The version of events hammered out by therapist and patient need merely be plausible to the patient and powerful enough to explain most things that come his way. One never knows whether any historical reconstruction, as made in psychotherapy or in any other kind of history, is an accurate representation of how things actually were. Indeed, histories are regularly rewritten. Yet having the feeling of knowing such a history as if it were correct seems related to sought-after change.

The Shift to Activity

Schafer (1976) and others indicted psychoanalytic theory, and the language in which it is expressed, for contributing to a technique that encourages passivity. So long as people live in the passive voice or mode, as illustrated by language that posits events as happening to us, we overlook our capacities to influence events. How can the patient change, he wonders, when he learns that he is the victim of powerful drives, complexes, early influences, and bad relationships; indeed, why should he even try when he expects psychoanalytic treatment to take three to five years? Bemused by the drama and discovery of the unconscious, psychotherapists have minimized the study of consciousness. We overlook, and sometimes deride, the power of positive thinking, the capacity to have things go as we want them to by intending that they do so and acting upon this intention. How often, when the patient says he understands but cannot do anything about it, does a part of us sink into dismay instead of moving with the patient into the arena of intention, decision, and execution? Too often perhaps — though not as often as the practitioners of the new human potential therapies believe. The new therapies have developed mainly as an antidote to passivity, one of their central tenets being self-responsibility. Gestalt therapists will, for example, adjure a patient to say "I won't" instead of "I can't." Whether or not psychoanalytic psychotherapists exploit this to its fullest, the assumption of self-responsibility, or the shift from passivity to activity, is another factor in the psychology of change.

Let us pretend that we are psychotherapeutic patients who have developed, by whatever combination of these change factors, a new understanding of ourselves, complete with new beneficial feelings about ourselves and psychotherapy in general. We are, nonetheless, faced with continual challenges from our familiar tendencies toward neurotic behavior and from the ordinary difficulties in living. What does the ex-patient do when he faces trouble? He may first dip back into his store of insight and attempt to understand what is happening in these terms. He may consider what his therapist would think, do, or experience in a similar situation. These reactions are the technological nuts and bolts of his new personality. Another thing to do, as Wheelis (1973) suggested, is to behave differently, to act upon hard-earned analytic knowledge, and so to behave one's way to further change.

But "action" does not merely mean large muscle or other easily observed behavior. Action can also include thinking, for example, bringing to bear points of view learned through analysis which make difficulties easier to endure or even to dispel through viewing them differently. Charny (1975) wrote:

> It is not simply the unraveling of their hang-ups that makes the difference, but a kind of constant focus on the joy and dignity of being oneself, even as one continues to suffer any number of upsets in discovering the utter insanity and absurdity of one's spouse, children, the entire world (as well as one's dear self). . . . the trick is to see these as the other sides of the beauty and grandeur of all human beings and not be flipped out by the unfairness of life. [14]

There is something of Yoga and Zen in this assertion that neurosis is, to some extent, a function of how one looks at things. As Schafer (1970) stated, a successful psychoanalysis results in a changed view of reality, a new appreciation of layered meanings, and a wisdom that transcends mere knowledge. Such a new world view may combine comic, romantic, tragic, and ironic visions. But whatever the specific contents, an enlarged and delineated capacity to experience what otherwise was narrowly, unilaterally, and reductionistically defined in neurotic terms can result in ways of living better, for which psychoanalysis can take credit.

Altered Consciousness

Here is a speculative but, to me, intriguing contribution to this list of factors in psychoanalytic change. We are currently learning from studying altered states of consciousness, as produced by meditation and biofeedback, that in these states of mind people have capacities unavailable to them in other states of mind. Under these atypical conditions, people control what were at one time considered to be involuntary physiological processes. They cause a variety of somatic and psychological changes by visualizing them, and they learn some kinds of material more efficiently than under other conditions. Such effects are not intended, or even attended to, in the psychoanalytic theory of technique. Yet the practice of psychoanalysis inadvertently may encourage such states of consciousness. The subdued atmosphere of the quiet, darkened office, reclining on a couch, the often soft, soothing voice of the analyst, the patient's quasi self-hypnosis from listening to his own voice for long periods of time all may contribute to the altered consciousness that exploits capacities for change.

One question that pertains to every pathway mentioned is the degree to w. ich it is cause or effect. Does intrapsychic change bring about changed behavior, or does changed behavior bring about intrapsychic change? Do the shift from passivity to activity, the capacity to benefit from a new interpersonal relationship, and the ability to turn mere suggestion into independently held and enduring aspects of self all bring about change, or are they the rewards of change?

Or is this question indeed the wrong formulation? Would it be more correct to think of an interaction of factors contributing to a synergy in which the whole is greater than the sum of its parts? In such a formulation, traditional cause-and-effect sequences would yield to a complex relationship in which no factors were cause or effect and were operative only as part of the total configuration. For example, insight may be useful only in interaction with the requisite amount of affect, both becoming useful only in the context of a helping interpersonal relationship, a corrective emotional experience, and so on down through the list of factors.

Once past the often partisan preoccupation with a particular factor, we will be in a better position to answer such questions. Nonetheless, one can hardly avoid the issue, stated crudely, of "which factor is the most important." This query reflects the argument that one often hears, for example, in the new therapists' denunciation of verbally derived insight and in psychoanalytic psychotherapists' implicit derogation of working directly on the body as a means of bringing about personality change. One answer to this problem is to try to rank the factors according to their effectiveness in general and to patient circumstances in particular. A sophisticated way of making such a ranking would be to control for age, sex, birth order, and therapist's personality and skill. With a valid ranking, the therapist could better emphasize a particular factor or relationship between factors. He could change emphasis during the analysis as different levels of experience and ego functioning become paramount. For example, as patients work with the more primitive levels of their personality, the relative importance of the interpersonal relationship is increased. It may sound complicated and would require a complicated research design, but I believe that good analysts make such sophisticated rankings and act upon them, sometimes without even thinking about it, to a greater extent than hortatory discussions might suggest.

Yet all these ways of approaching the assessment and use of the change factors in psychoanalysis may be largely or entirely wrong. The therapist decides in the confines of his conceptual world what is more or less useful to his patient. It may be that this formulation is only another way in which we have been led astray by working in the mode of doctor and patient. Could it be instead that there is no such ranking or that such a ranking is practically irrelevant anyway? Consider this analogy: A person is determined to go somewhere, but he needs time and money to do so. The rich man needs time, and so he sets about getting it from the environment. The poor man needs money, and so he sets about getting it from the environment. Could it not be the same with patients? People may have the wisdom not only to know what is lacking but also to know how they can best overcome these deficiencies. The patient chooses what is useful to him from the congeries of possibilities, just as babies and animals choose the foods that their bodies require. Perhaps all we can do is to facilitate our patients' choices by making sure that all possibilities are available. This function may reflect our main clinical expertise.

Our research expertise has hardly been extended in ascertaining means of change, as is made clear in Chapter 11. An obvious study would be simply to find out what the therapist and the patient think brought about change. This and other studies are dependent on follow-up studies, which are lacking at present. Without such studies, we are in the same position as the drug companies that sell their products without sufficient testing for efficacy and side effects. To rise above and go beyond that state of affairs, we need to know not only outcome—whether and what change occurs—but also how such change occurs.

Such a research comparison would, I am sure, yield much information about the nature of psychotherapeutic change. However, one final possibility ought to be considered. It may be that the full story can never be known with our present assumptions, hypotheses, and methods. Perhaps change in psychoanalysis is like creativity. We can learn just so much about it; the rest remains ineffable and mysterious. There is always the patient who, despite all odds, changes for the better. And there is always the patient who, seemingly with much going for him, somehow never quite makes the gains that we think he should have made. As with literary or musical talent, one can teach, inspire, and nurture in many ways. Yet what is produced seems to dance to its own tune and follow arcane rules. This possible factor in psychoanalytic change gives us no cause to stop investigating. Indeed, it should stimulate new directions. But it does give us cause for awe and wonder. Awe and wonder, too, may be factors to consider in psychotherapeutic change.

2

The Human Potential Movement: New Elements in the Process of Change

To those psychoanalysts who conceive of change in psycho-therapy as a function largely or solely of such classical psycho-analytic concepts as abreaction, insight, resistance, repression, and transference, the pathways to change noted in the previous chapter may seem ecumenical and exhaustive. To the practitioners of the "new therapies," those that have grown up in the last fifteen to twenty years as part of the human potential movement, the list of pathways to change noted in Chapter 1 may seem restrictive. The practitioners of the new therapies have offered new elements in the process of change and new perspectives on the older therapies.

Below is an introduction to these human potential therapies and to their views of the psychotherapeutic change of which they are expressions. This introduction should provide the context for the discussion of the human potential therapies when it appears in succeeding chapters.

If you or a member of your family needed psychiatric help or simply felt that life should be better than it is, where would you turn? This has never been an easy question to answer. In the past the family physician or minister usually referred you to a mental health practitioner whom he knew personally or by reputation. Such a practitioner might be a psychoanalyst, electroshock therapist or behavior therapist.

Nowadays, the problem has become even more complicated. Added to the conventional therapies is a wide variety of
techniques and philosophies, often grouped together under the
rubric "human potential movement." You hear about them from
friends, read about them in the popular magazines, or see them
on television. Their rise in just a decade has been phenomenal.
Most cities now have some kind of human potential center
where in particular young people meet, organize, and participate in the various activities.

Although these activities differ, they do permit the following generalizations: (1) Their practitioners attempt to separate
them from those of traditional therapy, believing that people
are fine as they are, but could be better. People are not sick;
they simply have not fulfilled their potential. (2) While retaining a number of conventional dynamic insights the new therapists
reject the structure of conventional therapy. Thus, participants
may meet for extended time periods at irregular intervals in
retreats, public meeting rooms, or forests, rather than in offices.
(3) The new therapists borrow heavily from the wisdom of the
ancients, particularly from Eastern religions and philosophies.
(4) The new therapists emphasize the here-and-now as opposed
to what they consider rummaging around in a past that cannot
be altered. (5) The new therapists favor feelings over ideas. In
their view, man has put aside his basic nature, which emphasizes feelings, for his later-developed abstract, cognitive one.
People respond and change on the basis of their emotions; so
emotions should be used to a greater extent than ideas, or ideas
about emotions. (6) The new therapists emphasize the impor-
ance of the body, its balance and grace, and the exploitation of its
capacities for action and pleasure. The new therapists consider
the person's awareness of his body as essential to the quality of
his thinking and feeling. Thus, the new therapists sometimes
manipulate the body directly, with little attention to thoughts
and feelings, and at other times alternate bodily manipulations with psychological interventions. (7) The new therapists
distrust traditional scientific method, even to some extent
disciplined thinking and writing, out of fear that these will

promote an intellectualization of processes whose main value is experiential and emotional.

Despite their indebtedness to ancient wisdom and to the insights of conventional psychotherapy, proponents of the human potential movement see it as the wave of the future. They mean not only to help individuals but also to change people's ideas about themselves and others and how life should be lived, to promote a "new consciousness." Such a new consciousness, they believe, is vital if people are to overcome their political, economic, educational, and social difficulties, to find new ways to get along as a society, to work productively, to establish the right conditions for optimal learning, and to enjoy life.

Whatever the long-range value of the human potential approach to the individual or to society, it is daily becoming too popular and powerful to be ignored. And it raises important theoretical and practical issues for traditional psychiatry as well as for society at large. In the excitement of Freud's discovery of the psychological nature of man, it may be that we *have* overlooked the importance of the body, *have* erred on the side of explaining more than experiencing, *have* restricted the efficiency of our interventions by the constraints of typical and traditional office practice, and have overlooked knowledge that is difficult to reconcile with the Western scientific method and the conception of man that it reflects. Or, we may be doing the best that can be done. These are empirical questions, whose answers, in principle, can be found. Too often, practitioners of the human potential movement are not only distrustful of a disciplined, scientific approach but also are inadequately grounded in the clinical and academic work, which they criticize and seek to supplant, to provide such answers. Often, those workers who are grounded in clinical and academic work are too busy, self-satisfied, or frightened to learn about the human potential activities. The result is mutual ignorance with the possible loss of enrichment of both; emotional debate between the two camps often takes the place of informed thought.

Each of the new disciplines, as well as the traditional ones, claims success. Apparently some people do change and improve with all of them. Yet it remains unclear which people are best suited for which approach, which method best reaches which particular goals, and what the beneficial elements are in each approach. Finally, if one were familiar with all the ways of bringing about personal change, would it be possible to design a therapy combining various elements from the diverse methods that would have greater efficiency than any one of them alone now has?

To answer such questions definitely one would need a grand plan on the order of a space research program. One way might be to recruit practitioners of approximately the same skill, train them alike in a number of disciplines, select roughly comparable patients, and examine the results along with those of suitable controls. The scientific literature on research in psychotherapy is full of instances in which this traditional scientific paradigm has been attempted, but it has produced equivocal and unpersuasive results. Such a paradigm may not be suitable at all for many of the questions inherent in this kind of exploration. However that may be, such a project could not even be designed without sufficient spade work in observation and experience and in comparing and contrasting the various disciplines conceptually. Such spade work is the immediate task confronting us.

Studying and evaluating the new diverse means of bringing about beneficial change are the major challenges of our time in the social sciences and helping professions. And it has been thrust upon us by a society that has become increasingly dissatisfied with things as they are and have been. This new wave of questioning, ingenuity, and hope ultimately may take its place among historical movements that were spawned more by wishes than grounded in the facts of human nature. Or it may be that the human potential activities are the cutting edge of a decisive break with the past and turn toward a new kind of future.

Whatever the final answers regarding the effectiveness of a particular therapy turn out to be, science and therapeutics benefit from the adventitious use of psychotherapy as a laboratory.

In that laboratory one can study and experiment with the many variables that can contribute to psychological development. Unencumbered by many of the traditional ways of conceptualizing and practicing psychotherapy, members of the human potential movement are offering new variables to be so considered and tried.

3

The Idealization of Insight as an Enemy of Change

The role of insight in psychoanalytic psychotherapy is a direct expression of insight's history, theoretical place, and technical use in psychoanalysis, which is the basic science for psychoanalytic psychotherapy. In this chapter I shall discuss some attitudes toward and uses of insight in psychoanalysis, which will provide a context for understanding how the psychotherapist and patient use insight in psychoanalytic psychotherapy.

CONTEXT AND ROLES OF INSIGHT

Freud's hard-won battle to show that a systematic understanding of oneself can lead to beneficial change is under renewed attack. Many of the new schools of psychotherapy and new ways of viewing people psychologically are organized around the following ideas: (1) psychoanalytic psychotherapists adhere to a rigid monolithic technique with all patients; (2) the psychotherapist does nothing except declaim interpretations (usually about the past); and (3) insight is far less useful in bringing about change than psychoanalytic therapy has claimed, if not harmful. Many of these critics are not trained in psychotherapy; in order to justify their a priori beliefs they argue against bits and pieces of the various psychoanalytic theories developed over three-quarters of a century, and they ignore their historical and intellectual context. Some of these critics may have needed to establish a professional identity not only apart from but also in opposition to psychoanalysis. Let us, however, move past an ad hominem dismissal of such criticisms and see whether raising these issues might be beneficial to psychoanalysis.

In answer to the charge that psychoanalysis is a finished and rigid system, one can argue that in one sense psychoanalysis does not require external pressures like those exerted by these new schools to examine and reexamine its beliefs and techniques. Psychoanalytic theory and technique are recognized in the literature as unifnished and as the object of continued questioning. Note the tentativeness, sense of ambiguity, and relativism in such remarks as those of Fenichel (1941) who felt that there were different opinions of the technique of psychoanalysis as "a consequence of the fact that the personalities of various analysts express themselves differently in practice . . . also because there are often uncertainties as to the governing principles which should be common to all analysts" (pp. 13–14). Greenson (1967) cited as evidence for his similar opinion Glover's questionnaire on common practices and the panel on "Variations in Classical Psycho-Analytic Technique" held at the 20th Congress of the International Psycho-Analytic Association in 1957. Nonetheless, powerful cultural influences have made psychoanalysts sometimes act and sound (and consequently to some extent think and believe) as though they were practicing a finished, prescriptive treatment. If one considers himself a physician or therapist in Western society, he is expected to make reasonably accurate diagnoses leading to reasonably accurate treatment prescriptions and to the delivery of treatments that conform to the nature of the illness. To the extent that such a cultural expectation finds its way into an internal expectation, it is understandable that there should be a trend toward an acceptance of "psychoanalytic technique" as is, despite one's intellectual awareness to the contrary. This is perhaps one reason that technique has lagged behind theory. "It is amazing how small a proportion of [psychoanalytic literature] is devoted to psychoanalytic technique and how much less to the theory of technique . . . the scarcity of papers on technique remains astonishing" (Fenichel 1941, p. 98).

One might also consider in this connection that psychoanalysis, especially in its early years, was a research instrument, a means of observation, at least as much as it was a therapy. This was Freud's position (1926b) and one reason why he was hesitant to let psychoanalysis become a medical specialty: "I . . . want to feel assured that the therapy will not destroy the science" (p. 254). So the skepticism that is inherent in the scientific attitude runs in uneasy tandem with the practitioner's need for professional certainty.

As for the cartoon view of the analyst who says or does nothing but interpret, much in psychoanalysis can be construed to support this caricature. This state of affairs led Karl Menninger (1958) to dislike the word "interpretation" because it connotes wizardry, linguistics, detection, and oracular utterances. The psychoanalytic process has been described metaphorically as a surgical procedure, with interpretation as the scalpel; as a piece of work, with interpretation as the main tool; and as a war, with interpretation as the chief weapon. Indeed, in reference to the basic model of psychoanalytic technique, Eissler (1953) asserted, "The tool with which the analyst can accomplish this task is interpretation. . . . The problem here is only when and what to interpret; for in the ideal case, the analyst's activity is limited to interpretation; no other tool becomes necessary" (p. 108). Roy Schafer (1974) wrote:

> According to the [psychoanalytic model], the psychoanalyst limits himself to making interpretations; otherwise, he remains as nondirective as possible. He neither instructs nor speaks personally. He believes that his speaking personally or emotionally will contaminate the analysis of the transference and that his instructing his patient will intensify the patient's resistance by encouraging the patient to intellectualize. (p. 503)

Merton Gill (1954) believed that "psychoanalysis is that technique which, employed by neutral analysts, results in the development of a regressive transference neurosis and the ultimate resolution of this neurosis by techniques of interpretation alone" (p. 775). Greenson (1967), believed that "interpretation is still the decisive and ultimate instrument of the psychoanalyst" (p. 39).

Now to a discussion of the role of insight. The basic model is, indeed, a thing of beauty: supported by structural arrangements and the behavior of the analyst, the patient is invited to say whatever comes to mind and quickly sees that he prevents himself from following that rule in ways characteristic of him. Through association to his current life outside the analytic hour, to his past life, and to his relationship with the analyst, the patient is enabled to see not only how he behaves but why he behaves as he does. Equipped with such insight the patient no longer needs to behave (or have symptoms) contrary to his best interests. The analyst's major activity is limited to helping the patient develop such insights through interpretation. This vision of psychoanalytic technique is, as Ramzy (1961) suggested, entitled to borrow Bertrand Russell's description of mathematics — "a beauty cold and austere like that of sculpture, without appeal to any part of our weaker nature, without the gorgeous trappings of painting or music, yet sublimely pure and capable of a stern perfection such as only the greatest art can show" (p. 505). With some patients the achievements that occur during and after such a procedure are remarkable, and what actually takes place does at least approach the ideal of the basic model.

Yet the facts of clinical life often fail to allow such a rarefied view, pristine practice, and gratifying result. Almost as soon as Freud laid down the basic model, which was derived from and designed for the treatment of hysteria, he was forced to introduce deviations from it. "Our technique grew up in the treatment of hysteria *and is still directed principally to the cause of that affection* [italics mine] [but a] . . . different kind of activity is necessitated by the gradually growing appreciation that the various forms of disease treated by us cannot all be dealt with by the same technique" (Freud 1919, p. 165). Departures from

the basic model were labeled "parameters" and discussed systematically by Eissler (1953). He noted that such modifications in
the basic model are necessitated by various symptoms, as these
reflect differing diagnostic categories and ego structures. A long
series of papers repeats the same theme: while retaining basic
psychoanalytic concepts and understanding we need to adopt
interventions to fit the varying needs of different people, and
some of these interventions may be vastly different from the
insight-interpretation matrix of the basic method. This "widening scope" (A. Freud 1954) of patients that psychoanalysts try to
benefit is said to have come about because the nature of people
has changed since the turn of the century, because patients nowadays come from different socioeconomic strata, because diagnostic acumen has improved so that we now can see the needs of
the patient in a more sophisticated way than before, and
because of the development of ego psychology and its influence
on technique. All of these stimulate us to design the treatment to
fit the patient rather than to select only those patients who fit
the basic method of treatment. Stone (1961) stated, "[the basic
model] is . . . more austere in the teachings and writings of
good psychoanalysts than it is in their practice." Why psychoanalysts should teach and write about psychoanalysis in ways
different from their practice of it is curious, a matter to which I
shall return.

Despite a catholicity of outlook, there remains among
many psychoanalysts an idealization of interpretation and
insight, as these are held to be used in the basic model. Schafer
(1974) called attention to a slavish following of the basic model,
an "honoring [of] the artificial and inappropriate psychoanalytic
model" (p. 504) which results, among other things, in a lack of
attention to other means of working with patients. Ekstein
(1959) found the temptation of some analysts to place a value
on the final form of interpretation, its translating function, as an
intervention "on its highest level." According to Ekstein, this has
been a "continuing misconception" among some analysts. In
"The Curse of Insight," a memorandum of many of the problems
connected with insight, Brian Bird (1957) showed that even after

emphasis upon the topographical model diminished, with less focus upon symbols and unconscious material, an emotional premium continued to be placed on the analyst's capacity for insight, as if this were the real and ultimate measure of analytic ability. Silverberg (1955) declared, "we have proceeded on the assumption that insight is a good thing for a person to have; the word insight as currently used among psychiatrists and psychoanalysts has 'good' connotations" (p. 532). A familiar task of those who teach neophyte analysts and beginning psychotherapists is to help them overcome the rigid, simplistic application of the basic model, so imbued have students become with the emphasis and value accorded to interpretation and insight. All clinicians have heard patients described as being "good" patients because of their ability to develop insight and to respond in a preferred way to interpretations. The implication often seems to be that those patients who cannot use the basic model to develop insight and respond favorably to interpretations are inferior in general, not just in this ability.

It is curious that on the one hand analysts have long recognized the need to depart from the basic model; yet they act in what might be called a phobic manner about departures from it, about parameters. The literature and clinical discussions are replete with anxious reactions to "deviations" (itself a word with tendentious connotations). These deviations are often advanced as bold, though they may be available in the literature and discussed whenever analysts informally share ideas with colleagues. Note, for example, the formal introduction of the idea of the "real relationship" (Greenson and Wexler 1969) some seventy years after the development of the basic model, even though Freud had offered the idea in his early papers on technique as well as in his last one, in 1937. Consider the discussion that most analysts have had at one time or another about that group of optimal behaviors perhaps epitomized by such questions as when, how, and if to offer Kleenex to patients, to extend condolences, to allow the patient or oneself to smoke, and to see a patient four instead of five hours a week. These issues can, of course, be laden with meaning and transference consequences.

I call attention only to the ambience of psychoanalysis, which seems to me to be one of fearfulness (and sometimes counterboldness) of doing or saying anything that may deviate from the purity of the basic model. Even such obvious interventions as asking questions (Eissler 1953) or the variety of ways in which one might talk to patients (Schafer 1974) have been underemphasized in the literature on technique and tend to be introduced defensively.

A subtler example of the suggested value judgment of the basic model may be seen in Eissler's choice of "parameter" (1953) as the term for a deviation from it. "Parameter," as a departure from an agreed-upon classical procedure or situation, is most directly and unambiguously used when it takes place less often than does the basic procedure. In psychoanalysis, however, parameters are departures from a clinical situation that nowadays is found hardly at all and in fact is specified by Eissler himself more as a utopian ideal than as an actuality. The nomothetic facts of clinical life would be conformed to better if the basic model were the parameter instead of the other way around.

"Parameter" is an unfortunate choice of words in another way. The schism that it creates, between the basic model and parameters, casts the problem in adversary and polarized terms and can give the impression that any departure, innovation, or even reexamination of psychoanalytic technique is outside "real" psychoanalysis. It fails to allow for attitudes, technical devices, and emphases that lie well within the boundaries of the conservative application of psychoanalysis. Some of these are already practiced by some analysts, and some could be experimented with and possibly adopted by others. As Ramzy (1961) has pointed out, "within the range of a purely interpretive approach there is enough leeway to conduct an analysis without sacrificing the basic tenets of the method" (p. 504). Freud (1914) went even further. To him psychoanalysis was defined merely by undoing resistances and interpreting transference; as long as these were done, other activities could be included and it would still be psychoanalysis.

If it is true that the basic model is idealized, featuring interpretation as the sole intervention and insight as the sole means
of change, then what may be the consequences? What effects
does such a value judgment have upon the theories of psychoanalysis, the way psychoanalysis is practiced, and the political
and social roles that it seeks to play, is forced to play, or is alleged
to play?

I shall discuss some of these effects and the dangers they
pose to the extent that the interpretation-insight basic model is,
in any particular situation and by any particular analyst, overemphasized.

SOME CONSEQUENCES OF THE IDEALIZATION OF INSIGHT

I will now discuss some of those aspects of technique and theory that are underemphasized, just as insight is overemphasized.

Cognition versus Affect

Outside its borders psychoanalysis is being subjected to
attack for being too intellectual and for explaining instead of
experiencing. Within its borders this is an old story. Reich (1949)
argued for a consistent intellectual guidance in technique, but
Reik (1933) was afraid that this would lead to intellectualizing
and would diminish intuition, empathy, and experience. Fenichel (1941) asserted, "there are doubtless some analysts who
would like to substitute knowledge for experiences and who
therefore do not dissolve repressions but rather play thinking
games with their patients" (p. 5). Fenichel made clear the dialectical excesses of the struggle between cognition and feeling:

> In the early days of psychoanalysis . . . the greatest danger
> was the Scylla of too much talking or intellectualization. . . .
> Ferenczi's and Rank's book represented a reaction against

this situation. They emphasized again and again that analysis is not an intellectual but an affective process . . . the authors certainly went too far to the other extreme. In their emphasis on experiencing they became admirers of abreaction, of acting out, and thus working through was the loser . . . in the history of psychoanalysis Scylla periods and Charybdis periods alternated and . . . it must have been very difficult to pass evenly between the opposite dangers. (pp. 99–100)

The problem was set for psychoanalysis in its very beginning. Breuer and Freud (1895) first seemed to believe that once the stifled affect was released through catharsis the symptoms would disappear. But the release was in words, and the words soon led to an understanding of conflict and the unconscious. The goal then was to make the unconscious conscious, to understand verbally why the situation had led to strangulated affect. "By providing an opportunity for the pent-up affect to discharge itself in words the therapy deprives of its effective power the idea which was not originally abreacted" (Freud 1895b, p. 40). "Abreaction, originally considered a curative agent, thus came to be employed as a technical tool in the process of acquiring 'insight' through interpretation with all its implications and consequences" (Bibring 1954, p. 749).

The elaboration of the discovery of the unconscious meaning has proliferated through the decades, while a psychology of affect has lagged behind. One may speculate that the intellectual challenge and excitement of the discovery that led to this emphasis was abetted by the self-selection of the verbal people who earned advanced academic degrees and entered the practice of analysis. A problem in training psychoanalysts has been to promote the recognition that verbal, intellectual understanding alone is insufficient to bring about change—that insight must be experienced emotionally. The difficulty of putting this formula into practice effectively was highlighted as psychoanalysis was increasingly applied to patients with pregenital difficulties, borderline personality organization, psychoses, and impulse disorders. It was further demonstrated as analysts pushed for earlier and earlier material in order to understand early object relations. Difficulties whose geneses were primarily in the preverbal years and presumably intimately tied with primitive ways of thinking suffused with affects were hard to recapture in the later developmental language of the secondary process, though unintegrated storms of affect might be made available. It remains for each practitioner to struggle with what is meant to any patient at any moment, by the rule of thumb that insight should be accompanied by affect. Each analyst has had to decide for himself, almost from moment to moment during a therapeutic process, when to stop finding ways of helping the patient express affect in favor of encouraging insight, and vice versa.

The relative narrowness of the range of affect with which analysts usually work was recently dramatized by Janov's primal scream therapy (1970), which shares important similarities with Freud's early abreaction model of psychoanalytic practice. Janov stated that under conditions of stimulus deprivation over extended time periods, shielded by soundproofed offices and especially as the result of a relentless pursuit of affect by the therapist, patients are capable of remarkably intense discharges of feeling. Coincident with these is the recovery of memories of intrauterine existence and the trauma of birth. Among the claimed results of this process are increases in the size of feet, hands, and breasts. If only a fraction of such claims proves to be valid, the question then would be, would psychoanalysis benefit from a return to and an exploitation of abreaction, whose usefulness has been overlooked partly because of the pursuit of insight? At the least we may discover that well within the range of even conventional technique we could work toward infusing the analytic process with increased affect, which, consonant with present theory, should better promote change. (We should not ignore the fact that abreaction can also serve as a resistance and that feelings can be produced spuriously for this purpose.) Although applicable, in principle, to all analyses, working with affect is especially necessary for those patients whose difficulties are decisively related to preverbal experiences (Blanck and Blanck 1974).

The following case is an example of technical error encouraged by the idealization of insight: A long-time alcoholic and drug addict was in supportive-expressive psychotherapy, begun when she was in a hospital. As she moved from the hospital, was able to attend school, and give up drinking and drugs, the therapy shifted toward the expressive end of the continuum. The patient became more adept at thinking psychologically and was considered for psychoanalysis. Hers were hard-won insights; she was neither an intellectual nor an intellectualizer. Out of enthusiasm for these changes and interest in the patient's increasing ideational productions, both the therapist (a psychoanalytic candidate) and his supervisor (a training analyst) somehow overlooked or ignored the fact that the patient was not keeping up her payments for treatment. She finally admitted that she had reverted to drugs and alcohol, using the money that otherwise would have paid her therapy bills. The patient's understanding and ideational productions were undeniable. But they were not accompanied by affective meaning appropriate to the primitive levels of the patient's ego organization and therefore were unable to sustain her through the anxiety inherent in the new challenges she was taking on. They were, however, sufficiently impressive to bemuse clinicians into disregarding what they ordinarily would notice.

The Existential Danger of Insight

What might be called the existential danger of insight is illustrated in Eugene O'Neill's play, *The Iceman Cometh* (see also Appelbaum 1979a). A group of derelicts, each with his own comforting illusion, is visited by Hickey, a traveling salesman, who joins them from time to time on monumental benders. One time, however, Hickey insists that they give up their pipe dreams and face the reality of their failings. One by one they attempt to behave differently but fail because of intense anxiety and return to their peaceful down-and-out adjustment. In his pursuit of insight as if it were a universal good, Hickey was unable to realize that self-knowledge has to be matched with the ability to solve the problems that once avoided, are now realized. Freud (1917) wryly noted that melancholics are capable of self-recriminatory insights without deriving benefit from them. Albert Camus espoused the idea that when one asks the basic questions about existence one opens himself to recognizing the absurdity from which suicide can be derived. Clinicians are aware of the dangers of psychosis and suicide should their patients be exposed to more insight than they can absorb without undue regression or than their environments can accommodate without untoward reaction. Careful diagnostic work, especially the assessment of basic ego functions, is required in order to identify those patients who cannot absorb unlimited insight safely. For such patients Knight (1953a, 1953b) recommended ego-supportive interventions as alternatives to insight. Guntrip (1968), in an object relations context, discussed the dangerous limbo in which one has to exist between insight and the establishment of a new equilibrium:

> The classical psychoanalytic technique is indispensable [to the solution of conflict. But] the result may well be . . . that the patient . . . is rather deprived of a main defence against the ultimate problem, the profound sense of inner emptiness . . . if he loses his internal bad objects while not yet feeling sure enough that his therapist will adequately replace them, he will feel that he is falling between two stools, or as one patient vividly expressed it, "plunging into a mental abyss of black emptiness." (p. 344)

A new view of oneself raises new questions as quickly as it answers old ones. The truth sets many people free, but not everyone. We may ask ourselves to what extent any excess zeal for insight results in taking more from the patient than it replaces or whether we act upon an implicit belief that if some insight is curative, more insight is more curative — regardless of the patient's capacity to tolerate and integrate it. As with Hickey's clumsy intervention, does the attraction of truth overcome considerations of technique and considerations of existence?

Research data are available to support the idea that for some patients with some therapists the development of insight is no guarantee of maintained gains. In the Psychotherapy Research Project of the Menninger Foundation, patients were examined before treatment, at its termination, and two years later. Based on 28 psychological test examinations of 28 patients at termination and follow-up, 7 who had done better at termination had become worse two years later. Three of the 7 had achieved the highest amount of insight on a four-point scale, and one had achieved the next highest amount (Appelbaum 1975b).

Meaning of Interpretation to the Patient

Silverberg (1955) believed that the good reputation of insight follows the recognition "that insight has a liberating effect, like education: 'and ye shall know the truth, and the truth shall make you free'" (p. 532). Yet Silverberg's patient, whose intransigence had encouraged these remarks, did not change his behavior. While pursuing insight it may be that some analysts overlook two other requirements for it to be effective. One is how the insight is offered. Just as a good script can be ruined by poor acting, setting, or lighting, so can the hoped-for effect of a correct interpretation be destroyed by poor timing, a clumsy choice of words, or a wooden or objectionable tone of voice. Therapists vary in their evocativeness, and one would presume that, all other things being equal, the relative effectiveness of their insights also would vary. This issue is discussed more fully in Chapter 6. Another variable that might not be controlled in developing insight is the unconscious meaning to the patient of receiving an interpretive offering, quite apart from the specific meaning, correctness, or manner of delivery of the insights themselves. The offering of an interpretation is the major action interrupting the relatively inactive mode of the analyst in the basic model. It is often what patients are implicitly awaiting. Occurring during the heightened emotions of the transference neurosis, these interpretations may be heavily invested with unconscious meanings that are often central to the patient's personality. Ekstein (1956) described the developmentally earlier meanings that are stimulated by developmentally later symbolic language. Silverberg (1955) reported that until he recognized the meaning to the patient of being offered insight, he was surprised and frustrated that he could not interrupt with insight the patient's acting out. The insight only became effective when the analyst realized, and interpreted to the patient, that the patient was experiencing the receipt of the insight as a disciplinary measure, which implied to the patient that the analyst was omnipotently able to assert his authority over him. Greenson (1967) also found that interpretations of the patient's anger toward the analyst, especially in the first phase of analysis, often make the patient feel that he is being criticized. Greenson offered a case example of a patient who had projected his impulses to be a humiliator onto the analyst and felt humiliated by the analyst's making interpretations. Bird (1957) noted that a too avid pursuit of insight creates an unfair competition with the patient and does not permit the patient to discover anything for himself. Although these difficulties may in fact stem from the analyst's offering too much insight too quickly, they can also be the patient's transference impression. Bird also suggested that some patients may view interpretations as if they were nourishment from their mother, and thus the interpretive work rewards dependency rather than stimulating growth. It seems plausible to assume that every patient at one time or another experiences the giving of insight in ways consistent with his relationship dispositions and psychosexual modes. Although one patient may experience interpretations as nurture, another may experience them as poison. Others may accept them as gifts, as something to be refused, as entries in a contest, or as attacks.

One patient who characteristically crossed her legs while on the couch resisted the development of the therapeutic alliance and, especially, resisted thinking psychologically with the analyst. She had fantasied that her sister, born when the patient was three years old, was the child of her father and herself. This child was born damaged and died shortly after birth, a fact that apparently contributed to the patient's fear of the consequences of sex. She seemed to have sexualized the process of thinking psychologically with the analyst, equating any insights that they created together as giving birth to an idea-child. Insights offered to her unilaterally were experienced as rapes, against which her legs were locked. The more correct the insights were, the more her anxiety and defensiveness increased. (For further discussion of this case in the context of psychological-mindedness, see Chapter 7.)

Insight and the Curative Effects
of the Interpersonal Relationships

A major finding of the Psychotherapy Research Project of the Menninger Foundation was that those patients who had developed insight in the context of psychological-mindedness and had achieved some conflict resolution did the best of all the patients. Yet, at the same time, a number of patients made substantial gains even in the absence of insight, psychological-mindedness, and conflict resolution (Appelbaum 1977a). The latter finding was a surprise to most members of the project, some of whom had formally advanced the idea through detailed predictions that the development of insight was a requisite for substantial, especially structural, change (Horwitz and A. Appelbaum 1966). Yet there is much in psychoanalytic theory, writing, and practice that would lead one to anticipate such a finding rather than to be surprised by it. Once again we might do well to consider the extent to which an overvaluation of insight, along with psychological-mindedness and conflict resolution, leads some of us to believe that substantial change can come about only in these ways.

By contrast, members of the British object-relations school believe that change comes about in ways other than through insight. According to Guntrip (1968):

> The analytical technique itself is more an instrument of research and of temporary relief than of radical therapy. The analyst's interpretations will be given to the patient as suggestions for him to respond to, not as dogmatic or authoritative pronouncements for him to accept blindly. . . . It is only the kind of self-knowledge that is arrived at as living insight, which is felt, experienced, in the medium of a good personal relationship, that has therapeutic value. (p. 356)

Contrast this with Freud's comment (1937) in one of his last papers, *"The therapeutic effect* depends on making conscious what is repressed. . . . We prepare the way for this making conscious by interpretations and constructions" (italics mine) (p. 238). Winnicott (1965) spoke of analysts who

> . . . deal with more primitive mental mechanisms; by interpreting part-object relations, projections and introjections, hypochondriacal and paranoid anxieties, attacks on linkages, thinking disturbances, etc., etc. They extend the field of operation and the range of the cases they can tackle. This is research analysis, and the danger is only that *the patient's needs in terms of infantile dependence may be lost in the course of the analyst's performance.* (p. 169)

The curative functional task to be performed by the real relationship is to provide a second chance for the patient to grow. "Object-relations theory calls for the analyst to be a good-object in reality, in himself, just as the mother has to be a good-object in reality to the baby. . . . He must, in his own reality as a person, bring something *new* that the patient has not experienced before" (Guntrip 1968, p. 346). Greenson and Wexler (1969), and Gittelson (1952) noticed the real nontransference relationship, though they stopped short of maintaining that relationship in and of itself has a curative function. But Edward Glover (1955) believed that many people clearly can cure themselves through their unconscious human contacts.

In American psychoanalysis a tradition of benefit through the interpersonal relationship has been asserted by, among others, Harry Stack Sullivan, Frieda Fromm-Reichmann, and Otto Will. A retrospective attempt by the Psychotherapy Research Project of the Menninger Foundation to explain how patients improved in the absence of insight was offered by Horwitz (1974); he cited ways in which patients may have used the interpersonal relationship to bring about their gains.

Psychoanalysts seem even to have minimized in their techniques their own theory of normal child development, which posits change as occurring without insight, at least insight of the kind encouraged in psychoanalytic treatment. (Ernst Kris [1956], who posed the question of whether insight had to be verbal at all, is an exception.) In such normal development crucial internalized self- and object-representations become imprinted into the personality. In interaction with such objects, the ego develops its functions, grows, differentiates, and consolidates as part of a process of continued living with "adequate mothering" in an "average expectable environment." In pathology this growth sequence is interrupted. Many patients suffer more from developmental arrest than from regression. Insight may be sufficient to overcome symptoms by supplying links between experience and by overcoming repression, but an interpersonal growth experience may be required to continue the arrested childhood one (Winnicott 1965). (How to continue a growth process through adulthood is an existential question, which is at least implicit in most psychoanalyses.)

Reporting on the consensus of a group of analysts on the treatment of schizophrenia, Philip Holzman (1974) found that psychoanalysis has developed as an interpretive discipline rather than as an observational science, and one with limited sources of information and adaptations of technique. In commenting on this report Donald Burnham stated (1974) that the interpersonal relationship is the major and essential part of the treatment, deserving to be understood as such rather than "being referred to with scorn or shame as a deviation or as a 'parameter'" (p. 193).

A 17-year-old boy had been a drug user and dropout from all other aspects of life since the age of 10. Despite the considerable disturbance implied by this and other aspects of his history, as revealed in his initial clinical examination and psychological testing, he was taken into analysis largely because of what seemed a latent capacity to think imaginatively and psychologically. Through the first year of treatment it was difficult for him to make constructive use of this capacity because, among other things, of his pervasive feeling that no one had his best interests at heart. For example, he would act unpleasantly toward his girl friend so that when she rejected him, as he fantasied she would, it would be because of clear actions on his part and under his control rather than because he was an essentially unlovable person. Although in some respects he made reasonable gains in analysis, he began to miss appointments and to provoke the people with whom he lived into wanting to be rid of him and the school staff into refusing to graduate him. He seemed to take attempts at understanding as proof that he was to be dealt with at an emotional distance, deprived of what he needed, and forced to conform to what someone else wanted. A dramatic turning point occurred as an almost immediate result of the analyst's finding, in part through dealing with his countertransference, ways to make experientially and dramatically clear that he wanted the patient to come to his appointments and that the patient's presence as a person was something to be valued quite apart from any meanings that might be attached to his thoughts or feelings. The patient again began to come to his appointments, he worked out a better relation with his girl friend and the people with whom he lived, and he graduated from school. (Without much additional work, interpretive or otherwise, he went on to college, got his first job, and in many ways treated himself better, all understood as stemming from first interpersonal, then intrapersonal, acceptance.)

Factors Common to All Psychotherapy

Some ameliorative forces, apart from insight, that occur deliberately or inadvertently in most therapies have been cited by major psychoanalytic writers. For example, Fenichel (1945) stated that "relative allowance for rest and for small regressions and compensatory wish-fulfillments . . . have a recuperative effect" (p. 554), "verbalization of unclear worries alone brings relief" (p. 555), "the very fact that a doctor spends time, interests, and sympathy on a patient's worries [may be] a very substantial relief for lonely people [as may] information about emotional and especially sexual matters" (p. 555). Glover (1955) found that "the psychoanalyst has never questioned the symptomatic alleviation that can be produced by suggestive methods" (p. 359), either by way of transference cure or as the result of quasi or inexact interpretations. Sharpe (1930) suggested the therapeutic usefulness of simply allowing the patient to talk with her. Writing about her first patient, a psychotic, she said, "I was too conscious of my ignorance and too frightened to do much interpretation. I listened for over 12 months for an hour a day to her. . . . By this very freedom to elaborate fantasy life, the patient got more grip on reality. *The foundation of technique lies there* [italics mine]" (p. 276).

Ekstein wrote, "the word 'correct' stands in our literature at times for 'true,' at other times for 'effective,' and often for both" (1959, p. 228); and "the primary intent of an analytic interpretation is not to explain, but to cure" (1959, p. 232). It may be that what is curative is the process of gaining the insight, regardless — at least to an extent — of its content and veracity. This would be a common factor in all of those therapies that proceed according to similar processes, a factor that is independent of much theory as well as of correctness (Marmor 1964).

Outside psychoanalysis, in a trend outlined by Rosenzweig (1936), systematic attention is paid to the possibly curative effects of factors inherent in all therapeutic interactions. These factors may function apart from the awareness and technical range of the therapist (Strupp 1973). All therapies may be helped along simply because the therapist behaves as if he believes change for the better is possible, that one need not be terrified of something unknowable, that there may be causes for behavior that are less awful than those the patient has assumed, and that someone else cares enough to try to understand him. The nonoccurrence of dreadful events could extinguish fears (in learning theory terms) which may contribute to the beneficial effects of a corrective emotional experience. The latter may come about inadvertently, rather than intentionally by the analyst as suggested by Alexander and French (1946). The placebo effect (A. Shapiro 1971) is one of the nonspecific factors held by Strupp to be "established facts" in psychotherapy. According to Frank (1971), common (nonspecific) factors in psychotherapy include (1) an immense, emotionally charged, confiding relationship with a helping person; (2) a rationale or myth that explains the patient's distress and leads to confidence in the therapist; (3) the provision of new information about the patient's problems and ways of dealing with them; (4) the personal qualities of the therapist, which arouse hope and the expectation of help; and (5) the provision of success experiences that increase self-esteem and a sense of mastery and encouragement of emotional arousal.

In all interventions that have change as an avowed goal, there is a self-selection of people who combine readiness and need. One can notice this attitude at various junctures in life, as in times of tragedy or major decisions; it can be brought on by works of art, drugs, or other means of altering the boundaries of consciousness. At such times we may benefit even from a friend's casual remark. When one identifies himself as a patient, ready to make the investments that the treatment requires, such openness is used to the fullest.

No one suggests that such common factors are solely responsible for beneficial change nor that insight or other means of change are therefore irrelevant. Rather, common factors should be assessed for their relative contributions to change. Such a point of view fits with the psychoanalytic belief in over-determination and in the complementary series.

Insight and Action

An important polarity in human life, and therefore in psychology, is that of thought and action. Some systematic examples are Jung's distinction (1923) between introversion and extroversion and Hermann Rorschach's (1951) "experience balance" (1951), i.e., Rorschach test signs of the capacity for ideation as against a proclivity toward action. "The thinker" and "the doer" are figures in art and in everyday observation. Activity and passivity roughly correspond to this dimension (if one does not look too closely — there is much "passivity" in "activity" and much "activity" in "passivity" as systematically described by Schafer [1968a]). With due regard to the grossness of the term "passivity," the basic model of psychoanalysis can be described as passive. In the limiting case, the analyst's one activity is interpretation; the rest of the time he silently listens to and accepts the patient's productions. The patient, too, is encouraged to be passive in many respects, such as in his recumbent position.

The basic rule suggests that thoughts passively come to mind rather than being actively prepared or selected and that insight, as a creative product, can come about through the passivity implicit in preconscious problem solving. Menninger and Holzman (1973) presented the heuristic model of an analyst whose unremitting passivity in the form of silence induced the patient to regress in analytically helpful ways. As analysts well know, passivity is not without seductiveness to all human beings, perhaps especially if leavened by the opportunity for authoritativeness and controlling pronouncements. Though this is a caricature of the basic model, it is not entirely irrelevant to the facts of the situation.

Freud altered this model in the direction of taking direct action that was interpreted to be nonanalytic, sometimes to further the analytic process and sometimes to depart from it. With the Wolf-Man he attempted to deal with resistance and advance the process by telling him that they had only a year more to work and would end at that time regardless of the circumstances. He also promised the Wolf-Man that the treatment would benefit him, a maneuver using suggestion rather than furthering the analytic process. Freud demanded that phobic patients face their phobias, and he called attention to those patients who made it necessary to "combine analytic with educative influence" and to "take up the position of teacher and mentor" (1919, p. 165). "I think activity of such a kind on the part of the analyzing physician is unobjectionable and entirely justified" (1919, p. 162). In *Studies in Hysteria* he has Fraülein Rosalie H. carry on a dialogue with a person important to her as if that person were present, much as would be done by a Gestalt therapist nowadays (1919). Freud was willing to "psycho-analyze" a child through correspondence with Little Hans's father, and he endorsed Aichhorn's maverick ingenuity (1945). End setting has since fallen into disrepute, although Freud (1937) was at the least neutral in his retrospective evaluation. His warnings about the timing of such end setting seem to have been taken as proscriptions.

A prominent objection to such activities is that they will

deleteriously influence the transference. Leo Stone (1954) addressed this difficulty:

> I am inclined to agree with Eissler that the giving of a cigarette to certain patients, in a certain context, might create serious difficulty. In general, if this occurs as an *exception* to a general climate of deprivation, I would believe it more likely to cause trouble than, let us say, an appropriate expression of sympathy in a tragic personal bereavement — or even, circumspect, component, direct advice in a real emergency which requires it. (p. 577)

By extrapolation, then, Stone suggested that the effect of an intervention has to be judged according to the base line, or background, against which it occurs. The more passive, silent, "classical" the base line is, the more harm might be expected from any deviation from it. By the same token, if there are various active interventions in the base line, then any particular active strategy may be expected to have fewer consequences for the transference.

I am not suggesting that all or any of the actions mentioned here are necessarily useful, and I am aware that such actions can be used without recognizing the countertransferences and frustrations borne of incompetence. I am suggesting that reasonable diagnostic and therapeutic thinking and research on such options may be hampered by emotional fealty to a passive mode of attempting to produce insight, along with the belief that only insight produces "real," enduring change.

To what extent does the analyst's shrinking from action influence the patient to do likewise? Rangell (1968) wrote:

> I have seen a wrongly moralistic, anti-action attitude which creeps into some analyses fortify the patient's own phobic avoidance of action and lead in some cases to almost a paralysis of the latter and a taboo even against the necessary actions of life. Such analyses may hit a snag somewhere after mid-point where a marked indecisiveness eventuates at the necessity to convert long-standing insights into effective action.

A common transference resistance is for the patient to try to please the analyst with insight and thus, among other things, to prolong the dependent gratifications of an interminable analysis. A possibly not uncommon countertransference reaction to this is to be seduced into remaining the central figure for the patient, basking in one's capacity to encourage the development of insight, yet all within the analysis and not reflected in commensurate behavioral changes outside the treatment periods. Bird (1957) felt that "truly good insight implies using judiciously whatever is discovered and correlating its use effectively with the patient's life, present and future, as well as past. Insight lacking practical applications . . . is not good insight at all" (p. 104).

A similar, if not more pessimistic, assessment of psychoanalytic practice seems to have encouraged Wheelis's observation (1950) that insight often does not result in changed behavior. He noted that change must come about through different means and quantities of energy discharge and that discharges through insight are miniscule compared to discharge through changed life behaviors. He implied that the analyst may need to find ways to effect such changes in behaviors. Without denigrating the usefulness of the basic interpretive-insight model, Wheelis called attention to its capacity for inhibiting analytic thought on how to produce change:

> . . . the haze of familiar concepts — transference, derivatives, resistance, working through, and the like . . . they are the useful tools of his understanding. Yet they have the disadvantages intrinsic to all concepts: to some extent they blind him. . . . Precisely because they enable him to view certain familiar areas more closely, he becomes loath to use his unaided eyesight to look elsewhere. . . . [The] counterpart to the principle that the patient must experience and work out his problems in the transference is less well-known, though equally necessary. This principle is simply that he must also experience and work out these problems in real life. (p. 144)

In this article Wheelis stopped short of encouraging behavioral change in the treatment session itself. His discussion was concerned, he said, with "the theory of personality change, not with the technique of therapy" (p. 148), and he worried that the analyst's encouraging or discouraging the patient's behavior would jeopardize what the analyst traditionally provided. Wheelis's remarks (1973) more than two decades later made it difficult to believe that at least in subtle ways technique would not be changed by his reformulation of the role of insight. After giving a case example of a symptom neurosis, for which insight would be necessary and sufficient, Wheelis remarked:

> Most psychiatrists know such cases only from reading examples like this one. Though other patients may have circumscribed symptoms, most of them suffer from problems of being, for which insight is not enough . . . the most common illusion of patients and, strangely, even of experienced therapists, is that insight produces changes; and the most common disappointment of therapy is that it does not. Insight is instrumental to change, often an essential component of the process, but does not directly cause it. (pp. 16–17)

Instead of the sequence "insight equals or produces change," Wheelis suggested that "the sequence is suffering, insight, will, action, change." In Wheelis's view, the patient must decide, equipped with insight, that he will act to produce change and that he must continue to act, for "personality change follows change in behavior" (p. 101).

Insight into neurotic conflict results in actions that renegotiate old inefficient contracts and promises (Schlesinger 1969). Schafer (1973a) took a similar position with respect to the actions that the patient takes, even in such "passive" modes as producing free associations and attending to the basic rule. The implication of these positions, as delineated by Schafer, is to question those aspects of psychoanalytic theory that cast the person as object rather than subject — acted upon rather than acting. Such thoughts illuminate both the human and the psychoanalytic condition. They suggest that psychoanalytic patients, cultural institutions influenced by psychoanalysis, and psychoanalytic theory itself are the poorer through preoccupation with the insight that is offered and accepted independent of action. According to Hartmann (1964b), psychoanalysis has an inadequate theory of action. An adequate theory of action would lead to specification, weighting, and understanding of the technical consequences and opportunities of the roles in action of consciousness, cognitive style, perception, capacities for delay and for making decisions, being responsible, and the subjective experiences coordinating with all of these (D. Shapiro 1970).

Insight as a Defense against Change

Almost any behavior can be impressed into the service of defense and can function as an inhibition to change. Conformity with the basic rule and the production of insight, however, present special difficulties in that they are what the therapists ask of the patient and in the right circumstances are indeed necessary. Abraham (1919) noted this difficulty in his paper "A Particular Form of Neurotic Resistance against the Psychoanalytic Method" in which he described obsessional, narcissistic patients who produce "psychoanalytic" material in the service of defiance, self-protection, competitiveness, gratification, and envy, rather than change. Fenichel (1954) found that "the patient uses a new insight, acquired by successful interpretation, for resistance purposes — that is, for a reinforcement of other repressions" (p. 557). That is, the patient uses insight as a defense against other insight, as do patients with partial or inexact self-knowledge (Glover 1955). Bird (1957) commented that "insight becomes an end in itself, to the detriment of the changed behavior" (p. 103). What analyst has not faced situations in which patients use their insights as a means of deadening their feelings or attempt with explanations to divert the analyst's attention from thoughts or behaviors that are not so emotionally isolated? Freud's rule of abstinence warns us against insights being used to analyze gratifications that slow and diminish the process. Such gratification may be produced by warding off further investigation, by lowering the motive power of anxiety, or by providing instinctual gratification, as, for example, in saying good things, proudly offering anal gifts, or competing as to who can produce the best insights.

A young married mother came for analysis because of her overweight and for a variety of other dissatisfactions. According to the psychological test study made before beginning treatment, she already had much intellectual insight. The tester cautioned that at times the analyst might assume that the patient understood things on the basis of her apparent insight but that this understanding would not be the same as that held by the analyst. The tester predicted that she might achieve many further insights but that it would be difficult for her to change on the basis of these. She would be less likely to be able to gain insight into oral disappointments and masochistic gratifications than into oedipal, heterosexual, and phallic conflicts. According to the test study repeated at the termination of treatment, this patient was assessed as having improved in a number of ways, although she seemed to be caught in an excessive struggle against unpleasant affects; and through her increased awareness of her fantasies and daydreams, her ideational activity had become more ruminative. As predicted, she had been unable to achieve the depth of insight one might hope for in analysis, particularly into pregenital issues. According to a third examination, two years after treatment, the patient was shown to be struggling even more with a decompensation of character and consequent troubled feelings, which had now resulted in a further surfacing of pregenital, especially homosexual, issues, despite there being no "noteworthy lack of insight." One conclusion drawn from another and independent examination of the analyst's participation in the treatment was that he had taken her insights to mean that the analysis was progressing satisfactorily and, for this and possibly other countertransference reasons, had not sufficiently sought to encourage insight into the more primitive aspects of her personality.

EPISTEMOLOGY, AD HOMINEM, AND OPPORTUNITIES

The traditional pattern of most sciences is systematically to relate new discoveries and reformulations to what has gone before. Consequently, it is possible to trace the history of ideas and discoveries and, especially, to know what is old, what is new, and what has been kept, superseded, or discarded. This pattern in psychoanalysis tends to be followed more in form than in substance. Much in psychoanalytic literature and at its academic meetings is viewed as if it were old, even though to many analysts it may feel fresh if not novel. Much is received as new when in fact it is readily available in the literature. What is known, believed, and especially what is emphasized in psychoanalytic theory and practice varies from one psychoanalyst to another, from one time to another, from one society to another, from one area of a country to another, and from one country to another. (One can conceive of this in general systems terms, with one idea or emphasis being forced by the overall system to play a particular role — the id role, the superego role, the orthodox role, the maverick role, the physical science role, the humanist role, and so on.) There are many reasons for this. In the long shadow of history the first 75 years of analysis may turn out to be only a preliminary phase, early convulsions from the shock of Freud's momentous discoveries. Not many fledgling systems of thought have had their early practitioners suddenly and forcibly separated and spread around the world to be influenced by diverse cultures, as were the central Europeans in the 1930s. Freud (1937) was alert to such varying cultural influences, as when he suggested that the movement toward brief psychotherapy stemmed from the rapid pace of American life. Not only did this separation (the traumatic nature of which may have exerted an influence) subject psychoanalytic explorers to diverse cultures, but at the same time it made communication and homogeneous development more difficult. The diversity of goals in psychoanalysis, as formulated by Freud from the beginning, is also an important factor. He offered both an instrument for research toward developing a scientific theory and a method of treatment that was as much art as skill and as much education as medicine. He pursued these diverse lines of inquiry, attempting to use the language, concepts, and ways of thinking of the physical sciences in which he was trained. Just as easily he used the metaphors of art, a Socratic teaching style, and permitted himself the sweeping speculations of an armchair philosopher, all the while drawing upon and applying his thoughts to anthropology, history, politics, religion, and academic psychology. In the course of this monumental catholicity, Freud operated at different levels of abstraction, which gave rise to different classes of words referring to the same empirical observations. He was enormously productive and continually changed his views. Each generation of psychoanalysts and, to some extent their students, learned different versions or different emphases. Finally, because of the nature of psychoanalysis it is extremely difficult to subject it to coherent, agreed-upon rules of research which in other sciences could serve as a referee or court of last resort. Instead, differences in psychoanalysis are often discussed at the level of debate, with data being collected by individual practitioners and subject to their idiosyncratic observations, selection, classification, inferences, generalizations, and communications. In view of all this, the fact that psychoanalysis has achieved what it has in therapy, theory development, and influence on the world's thought is a testimonial to its power. But such an epistemological background should not lead to certainty and complacency.

According to Eissler (1969), the many differences observable among the world's psychoanalysts are not great. In his view, within these apparent differences a congealed orthodoxy has arisen to the point that there is even lacking within psychoanalysis the paradoxes with which to generate continued thought. Perhaps the following paradoxes would fail to meet Eissler's criteria, but they seem to me to deserve attention: the psychoanalyst pays fealty to a model of work established for a kind of patient hardly ever seen, is encouraged to believe that insight is the single means of definitive change while simultaneously being encouraged to believe in other possibilities, believes in the consequences of affectively charged events in the preverbal years but is restricted to recovering these solely through verbal means, knows that explanations and formulations tend to remove a person from emotional experience yet tries to achieve both, and notices that some people change their behavior apparently as the result of insight while others collect insight and remain otherwise unchanged.

This ambiguity and fragmentation can be understood dynamically as well as historically. One would have to assume that all people, not just nonanalysts, chafe against the narcissistic blow inflicted by Freud's assertion that unconscious forces determine behavior (knowledge of which is gained as insight). The continuing hostility of the nonanalytic world has made it possible for some psychoanalysts to deal with their own ambivalences alloplastically. In a world constantly trying to deny the full import of Freud's discoveries, proponents of such discoveries may just as constantly feel the need to defend them, and to do so with less than dispassionate reflection. Such an impulse-defense configuration could be seen most clearly in the early years of analysis, in which acrimony and open debate were the order of the day. More recently, with Freud's insights at least nominally absorbed by the culture, the struggle assumes quieter forms. For example, a "yes, of course" attitude can lead to insidious intellectualization, a surface acceptance that minimizes the gravity of Freud's discoveries for each individual's life. The need for the ceaseless struggle against (broadly speaking) repression, which Freud warned against in his recommendation for periodic reanalysis, can be seen, symptomatically, in defenses and defensiveness. Still unsure, some psychoanalysts are chronically anxious about any behaviors that might resemble nonanalytic or antianalytic interventions.

A more specific, speculative hypothesis stems from Guntrip's opinion (1968) that "'analyzing' is a male function, an intellectual activity of interpretation" (p. 360). The "making" of an interpretation may be experienced as a phallic activity, as is implied in the words *in*sight and *in*terpretation, those *tools* of the metaphorical *surgical* and *military* trades of psychoanalysis. The historic hostility of organized medicine toward women is well known, as is the alleged "overtechnologizing" of obstetrics, the cross-cultural demeaning of menstruation and pregnancy, and the substantive position that "the repudiation of femininity can be nothing else than a biological fact" (Freud 1914, p. 252).

The basic insight-producing model is a form of technology, and technology is supposed, stereotypically, to be the province of men. Medicine has traditionally used technologies to buttress its professional claims against nonprofessional purportations of healing. We see around us now the flowering of various nonpsychoanalytic means of change in a nontechnological, often nonprofessional, culture no longer dominated by males, a culture whose emphasis is on cure and help rather than science and knowledge (Appelbaum 1979a). Perhaps not by coincidence these cultural developments have occurred at the same time as has the assertion of women's rights.

Many of the techniques and beliefs of these schools of change have been available to psychoanalysis from the beginning: abreaction; the real relationship; the emphasis on feeling, suggestion, and manipulation; the importance of the body as a means of influencing neurosis, as a carrier of memories, and as a source of information (Sharpe 1951); and the meditative states of consciousness such as "free-floating association" (Freud 1912). Yet these have been inadequately exploited, in print at least, and command less public psychoanalytic respect than does the production of insight. We may justifiably consider the extent to which adherence to the basic insight-producing model alone is emotionally determined by the wish to protect, exercise, dignify, and assert a phallic expression of masculinity, with the antagonism toward other means of change serving as a defense against, in effect, castration anxiety.

The psychoanalytic technology is not a pure exercise in phallic masculinity however; it is more like a compromise. Before the analyst makes his interpretations, he indulges in much passivity — listening, allowing, receiving, and relying upon "the female function of intuitive knowing" (Guntrip 1968, p. 360), and fulfilling the function of a mother (Winnicott 1965). It probably includes also the anal derivatives of overevaluating words while inhibiting feeling and action. Compromise formations often are protected by such defenses as unquestioning loyalty, isolation and dissociation, and zealotry.

One response to the possibility of "deviations," or nonstandard interventions, is a refusal to consider them seriously. This complacency may be expressed in open hostility or in shallow, patronizing indulgence. But those who take this position are acting as if they fully believe that the results they achieve with their present technique are the best possible for the most patients for the least amount of time and money. To me this is a breathtakingly bold position. A more realistic assessment would be that results range from remarkably good to disappointing. An informed, objective assessment would also recognize that outside psychoanalysis, techniques of impressive power are repeatedly being demonstrated with a wide variety of patients. It is indeed complacent for one to assume, without further investigation or trial, that such techniques have nothing to offer psychoanalysis.

Another reaction to the question of "deviations" is to say that analysts behave differently in their offices from the way they do in their writings or at meetings, that they frequently experiment or use nonstandard interventions without teaching or writing about them. Much of this chapter has to do with just that paradox, which for the good of patients and the development of science is indefensible. When practitioners do things in such a bootleg manner, they cannot be expected to do them as well as they might with a clear conscience, aided by the corrections and improvements that usually come from public discussion. Further, if what they do is in fact helpful, then their secrecy deprives others of their experience.

Another reaction would be to accept uncritically and use any intervention that holds a priori promise or yields intrapsychic or behavioral "movement" in practice. It is common knowledge that new techniques, even new drugs, are more effective when first tried than they are later. A restless search for improvement can degenerate into mere faddism. This is yet another version of complacency – that what one does is right, without its being subjected to disciplined questioning and experimentation. Intrapsychic and behavioral "movement" is not the same as achieving the goals of the enterprise, neither in psychoanalysis nor in any other therapeutic approach. One can become bemused by an outpouring of affect, a declamation of a new view of self, or a changed behavior based solely on an emotional glow or unrecognized suggestion. Fascination is no substitute for science.

A functional reaction to the ideas suggested here would be to consider the options and to select one or all for experimentation in thought and action.

1. One can give up or minimize the quest for insight (a) within psychological treatment by encouraging suggestion, transference cures, educational, inspirational, and cathartic methods; or (b) outside psychological treatment, as in meditation, yoga, or structural integration (Rolfing). Though not psychoanalysis, or sometimes not even psychotherapy, such measures may still be useful for narrowly defined cure and ought, therefore, to be in the awareness, if not the armamentarium, of anyone who sees patients for whom cure of symptoms alone, rather than self-understanding or thoroughgoing personality change, is the practical and appropriate goal.
2. One can, in principle, pursue insight and add to the process of developing insight other techniques, for example, allowing or encouraging patients to have sex therapy along with their attempt to achieve insight into their sexual difficulties, or allowing or encouraging them to subject themselves to the affective highs and insight-producing results of human-potential techniques. Although these activities might be used to resist and to influence the transference deleteriously, this is by no means a foregone conclusion and even if it does occur, it may, through analysis of resistance, abet self-knowledge and change.
3. The most promising option stemming from the wider inquiry into how people change beneficially is to try to increase the usefulness of psychoanalysis in general and of insight in particular. I think one would have everything to gain and,

if it is done with analytic care, nothing to lose if technical decisions could be made with a view toward such issues as have been raised in this chapter, e.g., finding ways to infuse the process with more affect, moving relatively from the "why" question to the "how" question, from idea to experience; attending assiduously to the meaning to the patient of the process of developing insight; being attuned to the influence of factors common to all treatment relationships; monitoring and exploiting the effects of the interpersonal relationship independent of self-knowledge; following up the stage of learning about oneself with the stages of asserting will and accepting responsibility for oneself; and taking action in order to live out desired changes in behavior. In planning treatment strategies, in making tactical decisions and in gently guiding awareness, the analyst might persistently ask himself, What are the relative contributions to this overall process and at this moment of the various means of change? Paradoxically, less idealization of insight may well result in greater useful insight.

Could such shifts of emphasis still be called psychoanalysis? If they are only shifts in emphasis, it seems hardly possible to withdraw the name psychoanalysis from them. In the view of Leo Stone (1954), for example, even more extreme changes in the conditions in the therapeutic process can be encompassed within psychoanalysis:

> How far can the classical analytic method be modified, and still be regarded as psychoanalysis, "modified," if you wish, rather than another form of interpretive psychotherapy? I believe that any number and degree of parameters can be introduced where they are genuinely necessary to meet specific conditions, so long as they are all directed to bringing about the ultimate purposes and processes of the analytic end requirements . . . to the maximum extent which the patient's personality permits. (p. 575)

After agreeing with Freud's criteria for psychoanalysis, undoing resistances and interpreting transference Fenichel (1945) asserted, "that procedure is the best which provides the best conditions for the analytic task" (p. 573).

Stone's remarks carry with them the implicit call for a diagnosis of each patient at a particular moment in time, under particular conditions, and with respect to particular goals. This, indeed, is the sine qua non of any experimentation, indeed of any technical intervention. If there is any inviolable rule in psychoanalytic technique, it is that the psychoanalyst should be diagnostically aware of the shifting weights in the influence upon him and the patient and should make his intervention on the basis of this awareness.

Finally, Ekstein (1956) offered a historical perspective on such rethinking and experimentation as has been suggested here:

> The master-apprentice method as well as the initial hostility against psychoanalysis have led to the formation of schools as well as to a vast number of special research interests which were frequently experienced by contemporaries as deviations and only later on were integrated into the total body of psychoanalytic theory and practice. The recent rapprochement between the "schools" of Melanie Klein and Anna Freud is a good case in point for the synthesizing efforts so necessary in all of psychological sciences. (p. 79)

It is ironical that psychoanalysis, of all systems of thought, should have to struggle to extricate itself from the effects of emotional and historical forces. It is fitting, however, that psychoanalysis, of all systems of thought, should as the result of such liberation, exploit the possibility of increasing the effectiveness of insight, of providing helpful alternatives to the starkness of its use in the basic model, and of more accurately assessing the capacity of patients to take advantage of and benefit from informed interventions.

This ends, for now, the discussion of those aspects of psychotherapy that may be underestimated and underattended to because of the idealization of insight. Another such factor, conscious intention, will be discussed separately in the next chapter.

4

Conscious Intention and Change

To many of us words like "will power," "determination," and "resolve" are musty and old-fashioned. They summon images of a newsboy working hard in order to become a success in later life, of Horatio Alger, and of the New Year's resolutions that will never be kept. If will power, determination, and resolve were sufficient to improve our lot, there would be fewer of us struggling, fewer of those gloomy statistics, and fewer patients for psychiatry. Usually we know how we would like things to go in life, but will power, determination, and resolve are evidently not enough to achieve what we want.

The demise of the "old-fashioned" conscious intention came about mainly through the discovery of the unconscious intentions that are outside awareness. We have learned that despite conscious intentions people sometimes behave opposite to their best interests, seemingly impelled to repeat the past. People try, consciously, to achieve certain ends in various ways. They take courses, get new ideas, enlist the aid of a friend, or change jobs or spouses or styles of life, only to find that the old difficulties reassert themselves in new contexts. We now are sophisticated; we know things are not so simple. We are no longer surprised that not everybody becomes a Horatio Alger. We even know that Horatio Alger was driven by unconscious demons.

Psychotherapists have long observed that will power, determination, resolve, and conscious intention also can be used, insidiously, as a defense against the exploration of unconscious motives: the patient asserts his ready-made explanations based on easily available, conscious information so as to make unnecessary the quest for considerations of which he may be unaware. He may take a flight into health, demonstrating that he knows all he needs to know and that his present capacities and conscious intentions are sufficient, so that further exploration is unnecessary. Gestalt psychotherapists, in their catch phrase "trying is lying," encapsulate the idea of good intentions as an avoidance of genuine intention to make a difference. Schlesinger (1969, 1978) pointed out that the child substitutes promises—his statement of conscious intention—in order to diminish anxiety, to neutralize what he perceives as threats from others, while underneath he maintains his conservative position of nondelivery, nonaction, and the maintenance of things as they are (1969). It is not surprising that we as people and we as professionals have learned to distrust the simple and obvious and to take a skeptical view of conscious intention.

But then what are the roles of conscious intention, activity, execution, determination, will and resolve? To say that they have no roles is to subscribe to a conception of people as marionettes, weak beings at the mercy of internal forces. Was the captain of his ship, the master of his fate simply deluding himself? Not really. The classic issue of free will competing with determinism attests to our chronic struggle to synthesize the two truths, that behavior is determined for and by that same person.

We have codified our recognition of self-determination in various concepts. Some functions of the ego are declared to be autonomous, to develop relatively free of unconscious conflict, to tap capacities, and to use energy in order to make decisions independently on the basis of conscious, known, and objective considerations (Hartmann 1964a). Moreover, what may have started out as being driven by unconscious motive can become independent of that motive and can achieve secondary autonomy (Hartmann 1964a) or functional autonomy (Allport 1961). Activities determined by drive can be transmuted into activities seemingly different from their origin in drive, so different as to be apart from ordinary activities, as in sublimation. Impulsions outside awareness may be so melded with conscious considerations as to be conceptualized as adaptations. Schafer (1976) reformulated the language of psychoanalysis in terms of action, thereby highlighting activity, decision making, will, and intention. Allen Wheelis's attempt (1950, 1956) 25 years ago to examine the roles of will and action in psychoanalysis is only now beginning to receive the attention it deserves. Wheelis distinguished between the old-fashioned use of will power and will, which even when one knows of forces outside awareness must still be used in order to make decisions and to take action.

The relationship between impulsions outside awareness and intentions within consciousness may be considered a ratio, much as Freud (1905) conceptualized the relationship between heredity and environment, which he called the complemental series: the more that exists of one factor, the less necesary it is for the other to exist in order for a particular behavior to result. Thus, a person with intense and pervasive needs may find himself behaving according to those needs despite his intentions to do otherwise. When there are fewer needs, then the person is more likely to do as he consciously intends to do.

As we read in the newspapers of apparently inexplicable events, or as we psychiatrically treat people who chronically behave differently from their intentions, we may be inclined to underestimate the numbers of those who successfully contend with matters and forces outside their awareness and who exploit successfully their will to have things go as they wish them to go. Many people, after all, do appear to make changes important to them by taking Dale Carnegie courses, reading inspirational books and articles (such as those of Norman Vincent Peale), or practicing Couéism or other autogenic exercises. They tell themselves, in one way or another, that every day in every way they are better and better, and they apparently are. For thousands of years, some people have contended successfully with unconscious forces by using the reassurances of religious belief as guides to desired behavior.

One could claim that those people who have been successful

in applying such teachings are self-selected, a special group that is capable of benefiting from this kind of instruction. Thus, it may not be the content of what is taught, or even the repetitions, reinforcements, and other forms by which it is applied, but simply the intention to change, which uses whatever is available.

Indeed, that is the point of this discussion. Some people intend beneficial change and act to produce it. Those who remove themselves from the unquestioning repetitiveness of unwanted behavior and take a stand in favor of changed behavior demonstrate an inner decision and intention. Their behavior is already different; dreamy wish has already been replaced by action toward its fulfillment. They are no longer going to tolerate dissatisfactions; they intend to be different; and they often demonstrate the strength of their intention by investing time, money, and energy in order to learn new ideas and practices. Various studies have shown that people who apply for psychiatric treatment and are put on waiting lists sometimes refuse the treatment when it is offered because they have already made the desired changes. It seems that the decision to change, as reflected in the attempt to get help, has already begun the process of intended change.

This point of view helps us to understand the effectiveness of placebos. A person's arranging to get and take a medicine signifies a change. Then, having taken a substance alleged to be helpful, he anticipates the promised developments. Not wanting to be disappointed, the person tries to implement them. Using this argument, one can also understand "suggestion," an often cited but little understood phenomenon. If one "accepts the suggestion," then he or she acts to achieve the result denoted by the suggestion.

One way of understanding the power of conscious intention is to relate it to a sense of time. Neurotic behavior is a continuation of the past into the present, an attempt to stop time. It takes place in accordance with the assumptions held in the past, made from the limited information available in childhood. It accords with the pleasure principle, which asserts that some things should not change, that pleasure can be maintained indefinitely, and that unwanted consequences can be postponed indefinitely. So long as time is stopped, one can in many ways act as if he can have his cake and eat it too. Conscious intention is a jarring bell rung on the silent conspiracy to live in the present but in bondage to the past. "Now," it clangs, "the time is now" if you really do mean to change. Unconscious goals, expectations, inferences, assumptions, wishes, and fears all must yield to the prescription that "only changing can bring about change," pressed by the sense of time as a force in the present. For some people, apparently, just the decision to change is enough even when it takes place outside awareness. Revelation, mystical transport, and conversion experiences are probably instances of this.

But it would be difficult to argue that in every instance, or even in most instances, simply the decision to change is sufficient. Besides the conscious motivation to change and the way that motivation is implemented, the more determined a person is to change, the less efficient the means of change needs to be.

One way the counterculture, or human potential movement therapies, defines itself is to oppose unconscious motivation. Its members vigorously resist conceiving of people as marionettes driven by forces against their will and as subservient, especially to the medical or medically inspired technology of psychotherapy. Rather, they believe that people have inherent capacities to "actualize" themselves. Even if they do this with the aid of someone else — a therapist or a guru — they should try to do so as equal partners, taking sole responsibility for themselves.

The counterculture's objections are excessive. They grow from a sociopsychological context in which people seem to require an adversary position. They fit with the human mind's tendency to go from one extreme to another, using dialectics to achieve new syntheses. On one hand, consciousness is necessary to psychoanalysis, and increasingly so. On the other hand, many counterculture activities are much like psychoanalytic psychotherapy. Some of their practitioners have conventional private practices, and all of them have, whether intentionally or unintentionally, an understanding of unconscious motivation.

Nonetheless, their position does encourage them to explore and exploit the possibilities of conscious intention in ways often deemed unnecessary in conventional psychoanalytic psychotherapy. As I examine some of these ways, I shall refer to Yoga philosophy, Silva Mind Control, Erhard Seminar Training, the Simonton approach to treating cancer, biofeedback, and Gestalt psychotherapy. For those as yet unacquainted with these activities, I will give brief descriptions of them. Fuller discussions are available in my *Out in Inner Space — A Psychoanalyst Explores the New Therapies* (1979b), as well as in the writings cited.

Silva Mind Control (1977) and Erhard Seminar Training (est) (1978) train students during two consecutive two-day weekends in cities throughout the United States and other countries. Mostly because of recommendations by satisfied "graduates" and free introductory lectures and demonstrations, tens of thousands of people have signed up for these courses. Both teach philosophies of life, attempt to diagnose and heal physical illnesses, and use exercises that promote altered states of consciousness. In these states of consciousness students are taught to imagine a screen on which they can project their wishes and the solutions to their problems, as well as ideal laboratories with male and female helpers to aid them. Essential to both approaches are the ideas that one can solve problems on the basis of what he learns in several days of training, and that conscious intention, aided by learned techniques, is sufficient for many life tasks.

Visualization in an altered state of consciousness, as part of an essentially meditative exercise, is an important aspect of O. Carl Simonton's treatment of cancer (1978). He asserts the belief that cancer is an expression of personality need. In group and individual counseling sessions, patients and their families are helped to learn the presumed purposes of their cancer, to recognize and to give up the despair that hypothetically led them to choose cancer as a way out of their dilemma, and to find other solutions. Patients also are expected to cooperate in a program of meditation-visualization and conventional medical treatment.

Biofeedback is the self-training of physiological functions once thought to be involuntary. Guided by information from machines as to how one is reacting physiologically, one learns to lower blood pressure, increase respiration, raise temperature, and relax muscles.

Gestalt psychotherapy, in many ways using psychoanalytic understanding, brings aspects of the personality to awareness through self-responsibility and a focus on the present (Perls 1969b, Appelbaum 1976, 1979b). Instructions, gamelike techniques, and urging all help patients to pursue changed behavior based on expanded awareness. Treatment sessions may be individual or group and may be long term, regularly scheduled, or on *ad hoc* weekends.

Yoga philosophy, separate from Western modes of thought for thousands of years, has recently supplied many human potential approaches with a philosophical base and with breathing and postural exercises and meditation-visualization techniques.

Basic to the philosophy of all these approaches is the power of the conscious mind. The est trainer asserts openly that the student will gain from the training only if he intends to. Those people who are sent by their institutions, are there out of curiosity, or have strong reservations about gaining lasting benefits from the training will not be helped. (This proviso may be self-serving in that any lack of success can be blamed on the participant rather than the method. But it could also reflect the recognition that people must take the activities seriously if they are to benefit from them, the same principle that underlies the alleged necessity to charge a fee for psychotherapy.) In a demonstration of one's power to control inner prompting, est forbids its students to eat or use the bathroom for many hours. What appears to be imperative need can be controlled if one sets his mind to it.

External "matter" is also subject to the powers of the mind, as in the Silva Mind Control's assertion that you can, by concentrating, find parking places and make traffic lights change. Ram Dass (1976), an apostle of Yoga philosophy, wrote that in the highest evolved consciousness one can literally move mountains. He is given to such overstatements, but they do illustrate the principle that people possess previously untapped capacities. Prominent among these are the powers of the conscious mind, such as control of "involuntary" bodily processes, piercing the skin without apparent pain, and other phenomena long demonstrated in yoga and now popularized by biofeedback and other ways of changing consciousness.

Yoga encourages an attitude of detachment, a tranquil internal distance from objects, people, and tasks. While one pursues this detachment, he stays apart from the "melodrama" of excessive need. He is aided in this by the ability to observe what he is doing while at the same time doing it. In such a state of mind he can accept whatever happens and can believe that every event is instructive. Est advises one to "take what you get and get what you take," in effect to make the best of all eventualities. As est explains, if you release yourself from assumptions and beliefs, you can be open to new possibilities. For example, if you can release yourself from the belief that one goes to the beach only in sunny, warm weather, you may notice that there are advantages to rain at the beach. For one thing, it is less crowded. In another application of detachment, est conceptualizes life as a game. We all are forced to play it, but we can decide whether or not to play it pleasurably, and we can determine its outcome.

According to Yoga, we create the world with our minds. Things seemingly "out there" are merely expressions of consciousness. We see only what we have previously experienced, we know reality only through our interpretation of it. Therefore, what we perceive is a function of our evolving consciousness. We are capable of transcending space, time, and the strictures of the physical and creating our own destiny. We are responsible for everything that happens, including apparent accidents such as a brick falling on our head. (According to Yoga philosophy, we should have been able to evolve our consciousness to the point of being able to anticipate the dropping of the brick and to avoid it.) Breathing and meditation exercises, along with self-study and reflection, are the means by which we develop such perceptions and abilities. Through such evolved consciousness we are able to control bodily functions, such as respiration, temperature, and blood pressure. Thus, we can produce and maintain health.

In applying the same idea of self-responsibility, Gestalt psychotherapists insist that their patients rid themselves of the word "can't," substituting for it the word "won't." According to Gestalt therapists, if a patient intends something, he can cause it to happen; if he does not, it is because he does not really intend it. "Can't" is simply an excuse, a refuge, or a means of avoiding responsibility.

The way to use conscious intention is to do what you intend to do. This operational, action-oriented attitude pervades all of these approaches. The sound of one hand clapping is the sound of one hand clapping, and it is pointless to attempt further explanations. Silva Mind Control offers tricks and guides to produce what one wants. If you want to create a pleasant environment, you should joke with waitresses and gas station attendants. Whenever you have a negative thought, you should say, "cancel, cancel." When anyone asks how you are, you should answer "better and better." If you want to live in a better world, just see it as better and make it still better. You might, for example, "mentally repeat beneficial phrases while driving or riding, before sleeping and upon awakening." You should also give other people "good positive labels such as 'genius', 'love', or 'sweetheart' rather than 'brat', 'dummy', or 'stupid'." If you feel anger, then "just calm down" (*Mind Control Newsletter* 1974). Many of the exercises taught by Silva Mind Control that help develop altered states of consciousness are done while bringing three fingers together. This serves as a cue to aid rapid "going to level," or altering consciousness, which promotes activities such as trying to find a "misplaced" (never a "lost") article and remembering names when meeting people. If you wish to wake at a certain time in the morning, simply intend to do so by setting your mind to that hour the night before. If you wish to solve a problem, visualize a mental screen, go into your altered state of consciousness, and produce the solution on the screen. Gestalt therapists have their patients repeat key phrases — sometimes to summon feelings, at other times to confirm, underline, and reinforce conscious knowledge and intention. In short, if you want things to be better, then decide that they are better or see that they become so.

Physical illness is caused and maintained by the powers of the mind that control bodily functions outside awareness and with little evolved consciousness. Since we are responsible for all that happens and can will how we would like things to be, we can heal physical ills. Simonton informs his patients that they are responsible for their cancers and that since their mind is powerful enough to develop cancer, it is powerful enough to dispel it. In Silva Mind Control and in est one is taught to enter an altered state of consciousness and to visualize one's health objectives. The student is taught how to visualize an illness or pain, to investigate it and open it to as many of his senses as possible, to exaggerate its effects, and thereby to rid himself of it. Simonton and Harry Edwards, a spiritual leader in England, suggest that one can visualize the successful treatment of his cancer and thereby can help to make possible that outcome. Cancer patients learn to meditate and while meditating visualize their cancer, the medicine they are taking, and their healthy selves conquering their cancer cells and ridding their bodies of them. Since Simonton believes that cancer is an attempt to solve problems, the patient is encouraged further to visualize his objectives for various periods of time in the future, how he would like his problems to be solved, and how his life would be after they were solved.

To many of those steeped in Western medical traditions, it is surprising that some people actually do cure themselves of cancer through these approaches. Such patients are a small group, however. Many patients when learning of this approach refuse to attempt it even though they do agree to such dangerous and painful procedures as surgery, radiation, and chemotherapy. They are willing to undergo these procedures but refuse to take responsibility for their illness or to intend and work toward enacting their own cure (Appelbaum 1977b).

In addition to being taught how to alter bodily processes through meditation, est and Silva Mind Control students are taught to diagnose and influence disease through psychic powers. These powers are held to be available to anyone who intends to have them. At the end of the exercises designed to encourage such powers, the mind control student is given the name, address, sex, and age of a person who has a severe physical disturbance. Then the student is told to enter that person's altered state of consciousness and to allow the person's illness to come to mind. He is asked to "cure" that illness by intending to do so, by visualizing the illness being cured in any way the visualizer wants, and then by visualizing the patient as cured. Graduation from est includes a similar exercise, with the implication that one has developed a new skill that warrants "graduation."

Finally, apart from illnesses, one can simply use meditation and visualization to feel better, to unwind, or to become more tranquil. In transcendental meditation, as well as in Yoga and other meditations, people do succeed in lowering their blood pressure and changing other physiological symptoms of psychological distress.

These are but a few of the procedures and effects of taking conscious intention seriously and of developing the conscious powers of the mind. The goals of these approaches range from the trivial to the life-saving; the explanations range from the simplistic to the complex; and the effectiveness likely ranges from none to considerable.

An assessment of the effectiveness of attempting to produce change in people is subject to many considerations that militate against simple answers, as I note especially in Chapter 11 and in my *Out in Inner Space — A Psychoanalyst Explores the New Therapies* (1979b). Clear and unequivocal conclusions about the outcome of such procedures (and even accepted, conventional ones) are, along with proper follow-up studies, still unavailable. As of January 1, 1978, of the 139 participants at Simonton's Cancer Counseling and Research Center, 55 percent had died; 22 percent of the 63 living patients no longer had any evidence of cancer; 19 percent showed regression of their tumors; 27 percent were stabilized or in remission; and 32 percent had new growth. The living patients have exceeded two times the national average for survival time after diagnosis. (But the national averages are probably based on a less medically well treated group.) I have known a number of people who informally claim to have changed their lives drastically for the better or have dispelled crystallized symptoms as the result of est, Silva Mind Control, or Gestalt therapy. Although patients' testimonials of therapy are notoriously suspect, regardless of the kind of therapy, that ought not to lead us to discount all such testimonials. The alternative, negative assessments, would be much less auspicious and not necessarily more accurate.

Within psychoanalysis, Wheelis's essays (1950, 1956) on will and action now are being implemented more often, theoretically and in work with patients. Schlesinger (1977) illustrated with case examples that psychoanalysts are responsible not only for encouraging insight but also for seeing what their patients do with that insight. A conscious intent to change can be manipulated by specifying the length of the psychotherapy, as discussed in the next chapter. Again, psychotherapists should move from a preoccupation with the development of insight to a relatively greater concern with achieving goals, whether these are within or outside the treatment. If the patient is influenced by these ideas, one might expect that he would do more of the treatment work. Factors inhibiting or encouraging his conscious intention to do so can be examined within the treatment and also can be carried over to self-analysis after treatment. Although the patient may not be expected at any given moment to attempt to get what he wants, ultimately the patient must consciously intend to demonstrate those actions and consequences that he claims he wants and to act on these intentions.

The line between the conscious and the unconscious was drawn after Freud's discovery that people are unaware of some of the reasons for their behavior. The line, however, is not as clear as it is sometimes heuristically portrayed. Instead, this line between awareness and nonawareness shifts, as does consciousness. There are forms of awareness, degrees of awareness, partial recognitions, and recognitions that matter emotionally and profoundly to a greater or lesser extent — recognitions that are available under some circumstances and not available under others.

Psychotherapists are greatly impressed by their patients' difficulties in becoming aware of a memory, a reason for behaving

as they do, or an explanation of themselves. But these difficulties occur under special circumstances: the patient usually expects that sooner or later he will become aware, and he may
also sense that if he cannot do it, then the psychotherapist will
do it for him.

But what occurs under circumstances in which the person
may believe that he will not be understood unless he himself
produces such awareness? Under those circumstances it may be
possible for him to expand and deepen his awareness, spurred
by his conscious intention to do so and by his greater freedom
from anxiety, since the process is under his control. In the activities described here more than just conscious intention may be
taking place. The application of conscious intention to change
may begin, at least, to open the person to the awareness of
information and feelings ordinarily out of awareness, ordinarily
unconscious. That possibility helps explain the reported
changes and is consonant with the psychoanalytic assumption
that substantial changes can come about only through increased
awareness, only through making the unconscious conscious.

Suppose, for example, that a person has been living a more
or less traditional, prosaic life. He then begins to attend human
potential meetings, has his body worked on according to the
Rolfing or the Alexander technique, and learns about and pon-
ders the uses for him of self-responsibility and choice making.
This person learns from Yoga of his limitless capacities and
opportunities and becomes convinced from curing a disease
through meditation and visualization that there are forces and
capabilities within himself that he had never before imagined
were there. He participates in est and Silva Mind Control, forms
an emotional group with them, and becomes a member of the
extended counterculture group as well, all of which support his
self-exploration. Throughout all this, this person reads books
and articles about issues, points of view, and activities previously unknown to him. He finds people with similar interests
who in sharing their experiences offer him opportunities to
think psychologically about himself and whose insights might
apply to him as well. As an apparent result, this person changes

his life, not only by learning and experimenting with these activities but also according to these activities, as what he learns generalizes to his work, choice of friends, leisure time, and personal habits. He becomes more thoughtful and philosophical, recognizes that he can make decisions different from those he had made in the past, acts upon this recognition, and deals with the consequences. This person's conscious intention to change can be regarded as the main fulcrum by which change occurs. But is it not possible that through the application of conscious intention this person has, inadvertently perhaps, expanded his awareness, and widened his range of consciousness to include ideas and feelings previously unconscious or at least less conscious? Rather than regarding conscious intention as antithetical or alternative to unconscious exploration, perhaps we should consider it as a possible means of exploring the unconscious, limited as this exploration may be.

A person who has never had psychoanalytic psychotherapy may seize upon conscious intention as the only means of salvation. Should he fall short of his objectives, he may berate himself and make a bad situation worse, overlooking the possibility that he might benefit from learning about influences outside his awareness. This person may believe that treatment is never necessary for anyone or for any purpose and may pay a high price for this misunderstanding. Further, without being aware of his underlying motives this person may pursue conscious objectives that in the end are inimical to himself or society. Suppose everyone learned to control stoplights!

The person who has had psychoanalytic psychotherapy may disparage conscious intention, believing that his psychotherapy "will do it" and that insight and explanations are sufficient to achieve his objectives; or he may believe that having failed to change through psychoanalysis as he had hoped, he now is as he is and can do nothing further to change. The power of the unconscious becomes an excuse for failing to use his capacities for intentional change. A person may use self-analysis in a similarly short-sighted way, reminding himself of his insights or even encouraging new ones, yet all the while overlooking the necessity of behaving in accordance with them.

In the last 80 years the pendulum has made a decisive swing from a simplistically conceived and puritanical belief that behavior is entirely under conscious control to a narrow, romantic, and dramatic conception of people being ruled by unconscious forces in the form of inexorable repetitions of the past. The pendulum should now return to a more balanced appreciation requiring exploration of the interaction between the unconscious and the conscious, between the unintended and the intended.

5

End Setting as a Means of Change

NEW ENDING, NEW BEGINNING*

A situation with an end in insight is vastly different from a situation without a specific end. Psychotherapists have long noticed the usefulness of the termination phase — that portion of the psychotherapy that occurs after an end point has been stipulated. In the termination phase, patients often experience and understand their reactions to loss and endings. And in that phase they have the opportunity to disengage themselves from their relationship with the psychotherapist. A task with an end in sight also has other effects. It can, for example, stimulate new material other than that pertaining to loss, and it can aid patients in making better use of all material.

The end point may be set by the patient, by the therapist, or by circumstances over which neither has much control. Historically, "end setting" is the term used for the therapist's setting of an end point, more or less by himself. Although end setting is often regarded with disfavor by psychotherapists, there are many examples of its apparent usefulness. Freud, Ferenczi, and Rank set termination dates for their patients in psychoanalysis

*Written in collaboration with Philip S. Holzman.

75

for specific purposes. For example, Freud (1918) tried to counter the "Wolf Man's" comfort when achieved gains were being used as a resistance to the analytic process. Ferenczi (1955) used end setting as part of his "action technique" to accelerate treatment. Rank (1945) regarded end setting as a means of intensifying the treatment by summoning the anxieties of separation. Dewald (1965) surveyed the effects of his setting termination dates with patients when he relocated his practice and noted that it seemed helpful in some cases. He concluded that therapists might "... consider whether or not the setting of a termination date is not a practice that might be beneficial to use in a larger number of cases than is the practice at present" (p. 124).

Orens (1955) reported that one of his psychoanalytic patients set her own ending date and in the three remaining months achieved considerable insight into the hitherto unconscious meaning of the analysis. In the following case, too, a patient set her own end point:

A young married mother, complaining of shyness, an inability to control her anger, and somatic symptoms that included mild obesity, had been in twice-a-week outpatient psychotherapy for a year and a half with modest gain. The treatment hours typically were stormy, and an attitude of calm reflectiveness was often difficult for her to maintain. At one point her movements became slow; she said she felt hopeless and worthless; and she talked of suicide to the point that the therapist briefly considered with her the possible need for hospitalization. She was frequently angry with the therapist and sometimes suspicious of him. She found it necessary to regard him as an "infallible Pope" and then resented his papal aloofness. When early in the treatment, she dimly recognized that the treatment and the therapist meant something emotionally to her, she could not bear the thought. She tried to defend herself against the idea by saying that it was not so and by having angry outbursts at the therapist. For example, after beginning treatment she had a dream in which the therapist's name and the street on which he lived appeared. In telling the dream, she sensed the significance of the references to the therapist and became quite agitated, refusing to discuss the dream any further. In view of these attitudes and her response to the therapeutic process, the therapist was careful about encouraging expressive work and in particular avoided emphasizing transference phenomena.

The patient had begun treatment with the verbalized expectation that it would be limited to two years, since her husband was working toward a graduate degree that would eventually require study at a university in another part of the country. During the treatment, coinciding with changes in the family's external circumstances, there had been discussions of the family's remaining permanently in Topeka. Sometimes she thought that staying was a good idea and sometimes that it was a bad idea. Usually, her deliberations with her husband about staying were relatively calm and judicious. One day, however, just when her husband seemed increasingly inclined to stay, the patient abruptly decided that she wanted to move to another city. There ensued a difficult period between the patient and her husband and between the patient and the therapist. The patient became openly suspicious of the therapist's intention to help her examine the reasons for her decision. She insisted that he wanted her to stay for ulterior motives. She told him that the only way he could be helpful was to recommend a divorce lawyer to her, and she told her husband that she would be leaving at the agreed-upon time, whether or not he came.

She planned to go on a trip to investigate possibilities elsewhere, decided not to go, then changed her mind again and went. When she returned, she kept up the same pressure. Finally, her husband made a definite decision to leave. During the next several treatment hours she concentrated on the details of moving to avoid discussing the significance to her of the contemplated move.

The therapist asked her what she wanted to accomplish in the remaining time, half expecting that she might say that she wanted nothing further and would stop. Instead, her behavior changed abruptly. She began to work hard at self-examination. From that time to the end of treatment, a period of almost six months, every area of her life that had been a problem improved — she got along better with her husband, her children, and her parents; she dieted appropriately; her physical symptoms diminished; and she acquired increasing self-esteem, hopefulness, and ambition. She formulated plans for professional training and said she wanted to have the same tastes as the therapist. The friendly aspects of the relationship assumed a prominence that had not been apparent before, and she was now able to acknowledge and consider it. Although she occasionally had bursts of anger during the therapeutic sessions, these were managed in the new atmosphere of trust and warmth that generally prevailed.

During this period, the patient had visits from her mother, father, brothers, and one of her two sisters, and she utilized these visits to test out the changes in herself. She had wanted all along to be able to establish a harmonious relationship with her mother and to end the bickering and bitterness that had characterized past visits. What she previously had objected to in her mother now simply did not bother her as much, and for the first time in many years the visits were pleasant and gratifying. The visits with her father, sister, and brothers were also smoother. She was able to recognize and accept the fact that she did not care much for any of them, a recognition that was accompanied by a feeling of freedom: "I am no longer a parasite," she told herself. By this she meant that she did not need to be a mirror image of her father (or her brothers) in order to gain their masculine strength. At the same time, she did not need to be attached to her older and favorite sister, who previously had been, in the patient's mind, the model to be imitated if the patient wished to aspire to "popularity," femininity, and warm feelings for herself and others. "They can live their lives, and I am going to live mine," she said.

The patient's dreams, and her attitudes toward them, may be taken as further indications of the striking changes that occurred. Early in this period she had a dream of being in long-term psychotherapy with the therapist and of seeing him apart from the interviews. About six weeks before the end of the treatment, she dreamed of talking comfortably with the therapist and his wife. She was able, without undue anxiety, to consider some possible meanings of these dreams.

How can one understand the patient's changed behavior? What was special in the psychology of this patient, perhaps relevant to other patients, which made the setting of a date beneficial? If the psychotherapist had known in advance that this might happen, what should he have done differently?

One explanation considers the patient's end setting in terms of her motivations, fantasies, and early life experiences — this explanation emphasizes *dynamics*. Another explanation is based on the meaning to the patient of the change from "infinite" to finite — this explanation is concerned with *structure*.

DYNAMIC EXPLANATIONS

About a month before the end of treatment the therapist asked his patient how she understood these recent changes. Her first reaction was to describe herself as a somewhat driven person who when faced with a deadline, organizes things very carefully in order to meet the deadline. Further reflections suggested to her that when the date was fixed she believed that the therapist could ". . . no longer abandon me, that I was in control."

She came to the next hour looking exceptionally well groomed and pert and began by saying that she felt good and "thin." She saw the bills on the therapist's desk and, as she usually did, asked if one was for her. She said she had been thinking about the therapist's question about how to understand the changes in her, and she was indeed puzzled. She became hesitant. The therapist called to her attention her asking about her bill. She then spoke about how important it was to her not to owe anybody anything but to discharge all her obligations to the minute and to the letter; thus, she wrote her checks as soon as she got her bills. Her thoughts then went to her sister, whose utility services had been turned off because of careless nonpayment of bills. The patient said that it would be "inconceivable" for her to do that. She described how troubled she was by the local library system, which indicated that a book was due on a certain date but allowed additional time before considering it late. The patient always had to meet the due date, and she claimed to be unable to tolerate owing even pennies. She said that she could not imagine not asking for the bill, even though her common sense told her that the bill would be given to her whether or not she asked for it. She struggled with the implication that her rigid way of behaving was a defense against the fear that she would be abandoned, that "the service would be turned off."

She said that she was terribly afraid to get too close to the therapist, to trust him, because if she did and he hurt her by rejection or abandonment, she would feel more pain than if she had remained distant. Her thoughts turned to the birth of her younger sister, a crucial event in the patient's life. She recalled many memories of how unrealistically trustful her mother was. After the "treachery" of the birth of this sister, the patient felt that she could never be trustful like her mother, and so she turned her back on the possibilities of identifying with her and tried to side with, and be like, her pessimistic, suspicious father. For her this meant risking abandonment by her mother. Setting a final end to the treatment, she thought, meant giving herself the chance to be free of the fear that the old feelings of abandonment, with all their painful consequences, would be repeated. She could no longer be abandoned; she would abandon.

In the following hours it became evident that this fear of abandonment was but a partial explanation. Along with it was the fear that she would *not* be abandoned, a fear that was fueled by the wish for unlimited attachment to the therapist. She offered the fantasy that if she were to stay in the vicinity, treatment would go on forever — "as long as I live" — or until something "artificial, external" intervened. If she asked the therapist about termination, she thought he would simply throw the question back to her. So in her imagination, patient and therapist would be locked together indefinitely. The idea of a mutual decision to separate felt to the patient "like a skit." What seemed real was being inseparable. It was, she said, like taking a taste of ice cream, then being unable to stop until she had consumed a gallon, which she occasionally had done. Treatment was like an addiction, she thought; she would be "hooked."

At times the patient could recognize this fantasy of the interminable treatment as a product of her imagination. But often she treated it as reality and buttressed it with "evidence": She had noticed that during the time that she had been coming to treatment, she had always seen the same faces in the waiting room, and she had never known anyone who had stopped treatment. She acknowledged having heard that psychoanalysis lasted three to five years, but she explained this information away by saying that psychotherapy was "more supportive" and that therefore such patients would require indefinite treatment. She was convinced that she would never want to give up the help of the therapist. Although she could acknowledge the intensity of this symbiotic wish, it frightened and distressed her, and she could think of no way out of the wished-for danger than to arrange an "artificial, external" separation.

The patient's fears of and wishes for a close relationship were traced with her to her past life with her mother, her present life with her husband and her friends, and her transference life with the therapist. The patient was convinced that she could not have close friends because she did not want to be "obligated": To have a close friend was to enter into a thicket of mutual dependence in which one would have to satisfy insatiable needs of the other and to risk not having one's own needs satisfied. She categorized people into those whom she respected for their ability to be friendly without becoming symbiotically entangled but who, she thought, could never like her; and those who might like her but would be consuming types like herself. The image in her mind of a consuming relationship, which so frightened her that she was driven to escape from it, was the one she believed her mother had had with the patient and her younger sister. The mother had always yielded to the requirements of her children and in the process had sacrificed herself. The patient put her fear of this kind of loss of self in these words: "To give to somebody in this way is not to be a person but to become a thing." The therapist noted that despite her fears of such a tangled relationship, she might wish for a consuming relationship. She acknowledged that indeed, she did have such a wish, but she could tolerate only one such relationship — that with her husband. One of her great fears was that he would become more independent of her and that she would be left yearning for this relationship, which "I need for any sense of security." She had to restrict herself to one such relationship, because she felt that another might alienate her husband. This seemed an important aspect of her fear of her sexual side, as evidenced by her inhibitions about dress, physical exposure, and social-sexual banter. Thus, she could not tolerate the possibility of having a close and temporally indefinite relationship with the therapist. As the therapy drew to a close, she said that if she had not had a definite ending point in mind six months before, she would never have been able to do in treatment what she had done.

Implicit in these explanations is the idea that by setting the end point herself — in contrast to accepting an end point instituted by the therapist or by accident — the patient gained a sense of security through the assertion of control. Her fears of abandonment or fusion could be minimized through the feeling that she was the one to determine events.

STRUCTURAL EXPLANATIONS

All human affairs have endings, and one may assume that all that goes before them is, to a greater or lesser extent, influenced by the sense of impending termination. Incompleted tasks sometimes create tension for their resolution, as Zeigarnik (K. Lewin 1951) showed experimentally. Completed tasks can be aesthetically satisfying. Last utterances from the death bed or the gallows seem to carry enhanced meaning. The final speech of a play rings with added drama, and the closing tonic chords of a classical or romantic symphony resolve tension.

Elsewhere I (Appelbaum 1961) reported on a series of patients undergoing psychological tests who seemed to have been influenced by the recognition that their task was drawing to an end: their last responses differed markedly in quality from those given before. Some of these patients seemed less defensive when giving the last response, as if they anticipated that they again would soon be in relative control of what they could choose to respond to. This reaction seems analogous to that of some patients in psychotherapy who offer material at the end of the hour that they would have been uncomfortable presenting during the hour. The process seems a variation of the "strangers on a train" phenomenon: people are fortuitously brought together and understand that their relationship is only temporary. Since they have a limited time together and the relationship is unlikely to continue beyond the trip, they can permit themselves more freedom to become involved with each other and to reveal intimate aspects of their lives than is usual between strangers. Perhaps this phenomenon enters into every treatment and to some degree makes possible commitment and frankness. The patient described here, however, could not be emotionally convinced that there would be an ending to her treatment, even though she had specified its probable termination date from the start. Thus, she could not fully avail herself of the freedom offered by being a "stranger on a train" until a definite final date was set.

Other patients in the testing series seemed to experience the end of the test as a last chance to express themselves more fully or to make their distress known. This was probably most relevant to patients who were aware that recommendations important to them would be made partly on the basis of testing. But it is possible that all people have a wish to make themselves known as fully as possible and to have experiences previously denied them. This is likely to be particularly true when a patient has embarked on a treatment procedure that specifies itself, implicitly and explicitly, as at least one occasion at which the patient may involve and unburden himself without the fears and demands usually inherent in other human relationships.

Changed perspectives of time, as well as an atmosphere of acceptance, contribute to such freedom. In the Japanese movie *Ikuru*, when a dull bureaucrat is told that he will die in six months, he sets about sampling the kinds of life he had previously ignored. We (1962) have suggested that to suicidal patients the misery and hopelessness of the present seem indefinite and immutable. One way of viewing the fantasy held by the patient discussed here — that there could be no separation from the therapist and that she and the therapist would go on forever — suggests that her perspective of time was limited and constricted. Her wish for interminability (and the associated fear) was so strong as to distort her experience of time. The fixed termination apparently forcibly reinstated her awareness that human events have an ending as well as a beginning. Only then was she able to express hitherto rigidly restricted ideas and to permit herself to be aware of experiences previously unavailable to her.

If there had been no extrinsic reason for the patient's leaving the area and if the therapist himself had taken the initiative in setting the termination date in the midst of the treatment, such an apparently good result may not have occurred. The psychological situation would have been different. The patient would have lacked the advantages accruing from an increased feeling of control. Her fear of consuming closeness, presumably, would have been allayed; but her fear of abandonment possibly would have been confirmed, with its consequent self-directed hatred, further loss of self-esteem, and bitterness toward others.

ENDING AT THE BEGINNING

A 37-year-old mother of two, an overweight ex-schoolteacher, had undertaken psychotherapy because of marital troubles, and now the treatment had come to an end. She was grateful to the therapist for the help he had given her, for being the one person in her life who had listened uncritically to and understood her, and she was tearfully unhappy at leaving him. At the same time, she recognized her anger at him for, among other things, allowing the treatment to end.

During therapy, the patient had learned about the central conflicts in her life: how she had fought and stifled the identity of a striving, capable person because of the need to subjugate herself to her husband; how she had bottled up her anger and renounced her desires because she feared that otherwise he would leave her. She had recognized how such feelings and conflicts affected her relationship with her husband and children and was able to see that this was a continuation of her past relationship with her mother. Her mother, too, had done the patient's thinking, made her decisions, and controlled her life, something the patient had felt she needed at the time. Now she saw that she had both needed and resented it but had been afraid of retaliation should her mother learn how resentful she was. At times she had wished her mother dead. She had experienced intensely in the treatment her terrified and lonely self. Her resistances came up mainly when she was about to feel the anger that in fantasy would result in such lonely terror. Eating had been one way of reassuring herself that she would never have to be entirely alone and without sustenance. While working with this material she had given up a peculiar digestive symptom, though she had not fully conquered the temptation to overeat. She was now able to set plans in motion to further her education in order to continue her career; and she could feel, despite occasional misgivings, that she had the right to take time and money from the family in order to do what was necessary for herself. She realized that her conflicts were not entirely resolved but felt that her new awareness of them would help her not to give in to them as she continued to improve the quality of her life. In short, this patient and her therapist had ended their work feeling reasonably satisfied with a job seemingly well done.

This state of affairs at the end of a treatment is doubtless familiar to most psychotherapists, except for one thing. Agreed upon beforehand, the time of the treatment, from initial consultation to the last meeting, was nine hours. During the last hour, the patient said, "I had to work hard because I had so little time."

A 13-year-old patient in psychoanalysis, immediately after an ending date was agreed upon, said, "I have to say things now, I can't put them off until tomorrow." And "I have to stop cutting off my nose to spite my face."

A woman had been treated for drinking and obsessional thoughts in a dynamically oriented psychiatric hospital for six months without having involved herself psychologically. Several years later she returned with the same complaints for a one-week outpatient examination. Afterward, she reported to her husband, "I have gotten more from this one week than from my whole previous hospitalization." She did, indeed, surprise everyone with her ability to think psychologically and with other improved behaviors commensurate with her statement.

I suggest that these three patients were at least in part responding to Parkinson's Law (Parkinson 1957), a social critic's droll statement of a profound observation: we shrink the time necesary to perform a task when little time is available or expand the time work takes when more time is available. According to Parkinson, the time needed to produce a result is subject to factors other than those inherent in the task itself.

If a patient goes to a surgeon he can rightfully expect the "procedure" to take a predictable amount of time and to be so informed. This prediction is based upon past experience with people much like the patient in question and upon the implicit assumption that the procedure be completed as quickly as possible. Any variations would be due only to the hasty or leisurely attitude of the practitioner, or unexpected complications with the patient.

None of these latter considerations applies very well to psychotherapy. Our diagnostic criteria are usually not fine enough to allow highly differentiated, accurate predictions of how long it will take any one person to solve his problem. The prescribed operations are abstract. Most important, the doer usually turns out not to be the practitioner and expert, the one who has a backlog of experience and precedent, but the patient. This is usually the patient's one and only "case," he "flies at night," and responds to whatever buffeting and landmarks he encounters. Could it not be that one of these flying conditions is the amount of time scheduled for his trip and that all patients unconsciously pace themselves according to their expectations of their time in psychotherapy, just as people do with all other tasks?

A fixed time limit entails influences inherent in beginnings, middles, and ends. The patients have almost a palpable sense of where in the process they are—the process has tonus (Phllips and Johnston 1954). Some people start fast and slow up, and others find it difficult to begin but gather momentum as the treatment proceeds. Still others settle into what they experience as the real business in the middle, in contrast to those who get bored in the extended middle of things.

Endings, however, probably have the greatest psychological impact. Most people have noticed that when they are carrying something at the limit of their strength, they often are able to carry it just to their destination; only when the destination is reached do they drop it. It is too much of a coincidence to think that the time and distance they have been carrying it correspond exactly to the outer physical limit of their ability. Rather, it is more likely that the meaning of the ending of the task is decisive—for example, having proved oneself, relief, or anger at having had to work so hard. The perennial question, "If you had only a year to live, what would you do?" reflects an implicit awareness that a person's view of his life, his goals, and himself all change when the end is in sight.

An understanding of endings requires that we consider the existential meaning of time, and that requires us to deal with death. The calendar measures our lives. As the therapist literally or figuratively turns the calendar's pages, the patient, unconsciously at least, hopes that the therapist will never find the last page. Saying good-by, surmounting loss, and bringing things to a conclusion are among the most difficult tasks we are asked to perform, as patients and as people. We fight these tasks as we fight the reality principle. We are quick to believe that all good things will come sooner or later, that the therapist has the magic that our mother did in the endless beginning before time was invented for us. This is as true of the procrastinator as it is of the punctual person; of the independent, skeptical pessimist as it is of the clinging, believing optimist. As we are subject to the wish for endless mothering, so must we all come to terms with the father's later rule-giving entry. Death is a male carrying a scythe (B. Lewin 1952). This is the source of our "time horror" (Mann 1973).

When we set the time and sound the existential echoes, separation and individuation become prominent, as noted by Mann (1973) and Langs (1974). Is such a bias artificial and diversionary? It seems not to be. Rather, separation and individuation, universally important developmental issues in themselves, become elaborated in the treatment, according to each individual's central conflicts, defenses, and character.

Character often encapsulates content. The characteristic way a patient reacts to the short time allotted or to the imminence of ending provides information whose interpretation is crucial.

A psychotically depressed woman in a 16-week psychotherapy reacted emotionally throughout that time to its stipulated length. She showed an inability to organize most of her thoughts temporally, with past events appearing as if they had just taken place and current ones appearing to be from the past. One of this patient's central underlying difficulties was her inability to achieve liberation through mourning. The challenges began (so far as could be ascertained in this therapy) with the death of her father when she was 14 and included the death of her husband a decade before the treatment. She had become especially upset when some payments from his estate expired; this seemed to confront her with the reality of his death. Unable to recognize her anger toward these lost people, she could not mourn them well enough to allow the relationships to end. Her turning her anger against herself, instead, was the major focus of interpretations during the treatment, especially as linked to the therapist and to the ending that she so bitterly resisted. In the next to the last hour she remarked that she was confident that since the therapist had not recommended drugs, then drugs could not be useful to her. Shortly afterward, she said that she liked the therapist so much she could not be angry about his setting the time limit. He (again) said that she had great difficulty believing that she could like him, yet be angry and disagree with him and that this is what made it difficult for her to come to terms with her losses. She said that she had idealized her father in the same way that she had idealized her husband and the therapist and, in the process, had denied her anger at her father. She recalled, for example, that she resented his forcing her to take piano lessons and implying that she had to be good at it in order to have his love. She revealed that she had just thrown out her dead husband's letters, something she had wanted to do for many years but had felt too guilty to do.

A perennial question for psychotherapists is why patients fail to change, even though they seem to have developed an understanding of those aspects of themselves that probably are preventing change. The explanation often given is that understanding in and of itself is insufficient, that conflicts must be resolved, and that material must be worked through. Another possibility, however, is that understanding does not result directly in change at all. For example, it may be an effect of change rather than a cause. As Allen Wheelis (1950, 1956) pointed out, interspersed between understanding and changed behavior is the will to put the behavior into practice and to take the actions that do produce and consolidate change. This point is at least implicit in Roy Schafer's emphasis (1973a) upon the patient as doer and intender — the often unwilling but decisive bearer of responsibility. However, if the patient assumes that changes are going to take, for example, three years, even if he should develop adequate understanding earlier, he may not realize that he has the option to employ will and take action then and there. Why should he, when change is not supposed to come for a long time yet, and anyway (some patients feel) given the requisite amount of time, the treatment will do it for them? It makes more sense to employ will and action in order to enact change when the expected time comes to do so. Thus, the self-fulfilling prophecy is indeed fulfilled — change comes just about the time that it was assumed from the beginning that it would. (It should be understood that "action" in this context need not refer solely to easily observed behavior. Action, or movement, can take place intrapsychically.)

Many therapists fear that instead of responding to a time limit with more information or faster movement, a patient will take advantage of the known end point to withhold himself and remain unchanged, aware that if he can just hold on long enough, he will be free of challenges and tension. This can occur. Or he might change his behavior so as to convince himself and the therapist that no more work needs to be done, in or out of treatment; and there would not be time for this "flight into health" to collapse of its own weight, which often happens in long-term, open-ended treatment. As with any resistance, the effect of abusing the time limit depends upon whether the therapist can help the patient to learn about it and give it up. It may be that with less time available, analyzing the resistances would be more difficult. Or, it may be that with less time this task would go faster. Although some resistances might be encouraged by realizing the finiteness of time, others might be alleviated.

In open-ended psychotherapy, the therapist has to cope with the resistance made possible by timelessness, the impression the patient may have that he need not bring up or work with certain material or make changes on the basis of it at any particular point, since there is in effect no hurry. In such situations the therapist has to find ways of experientially reminding the patient that theirs is not an isolated activity but part of life and that life is passing by. With the end preordained, neither the therapist nor the patient can comfort himself with the feeling that there is always more time and that around some corner will appear the ultimately effective insights, memories, or feelings.

At first I was startled by how much benefit some patients seemed to derive from few sessions, as with the cases reported here. But for several reasons there should have been no need for me to be startled at all. Through the years I have observed that the same predictable patterns emerge in groups whether the groups meet for a few hours or a few years (Appelbaum 1963, 1966a, 1967). At the Menninger Foundation people come long distances for intensive outpatient examinations, which may last several days to two weeks; a local observation is that predictable beginnings, middles, and ends occur in these situations, and often there is a remarkable amount of change during these brief examinations. On the basis of his research on brief psychotherapy, Malan (1963) became favorably disposed to the idea of setting a time limit in advance — and found that his patients derived much benefit from such brief interventions. Occupational characteristics, if not hazards, of being a psychotherapist may contribute to the surprise or disbelief at such a notion as Parkinson's Law being applied to psychological treatment. Such disbelief may stem in part from the psychotherapist's theory and experience with the power of the unconscious, an unconscious that is so often unresponsive to common-sense ideas and homely considerations. Some psychoanalytic writings offer a conception of an unconscious that proceeds at its own pace and that one finds difficult to interfere with helpfully except in classical, technical ways. The delivery of material to consciousness through couch-induced relaxation and letting thoughts come to mind in an atmosphere of evenly hovering attention are passive modes which are compatible with the unconscious taking all the time that it needs. By contrast many expensive years of treatment implies, if not forces, time-consuming perfectionism. The increasing preoccupation with deeper and earlier experiences stems naturally from such a contract and goal. The exceptions to the standard conditions of psychoanalysis are labeled as parameters, a term that means, after all, departures from an agreed-upon classical system. The classical way of working is sometimes exalted, even though it is inappropriate for many clinical problems. Therefore, psychotherapists may collude with the patient's motives in extending treatment beyond the time it might otherwise take if a more pointed, problem-solving attitude were adopted, as instigated and dramatized by setting a time limit.

Malan (1963) found in his research group's cases that the willingness and ability of the patient to become deeply involved, matched by the therapist's enthusiasm, were essential to producing satisfactory results. Hard work and enthusiasm are easier to sustain when the end is in sight and thus are stimulated when the ending is agreed upon at the beginning of treatment. The longer the stipulated time, the less the effect, though even a distant end point may still be better than none at all, and it could serve to counter the apathy and routinization to which seemingly endless tasks are susceptible. I had originally recommended long-term psychotherapy to the overweight mother and ex-schoolteacher. But she insisted that she wanted to spend only a few hours talking with me. Once I agreed to this, she showed a high degree of willingness and energy in the psychotherapy. And despite the failure of my initial recommendation, I was enthusiastic about working with her, responding to her psychological-mindedness, and sharing her determination to see what could be accomplished in the short amount of time we allotted ourselves.

In addition to setting the brief time limit, I restricted "free" associations in favor of attending to a focal conflict, which was selected as having at least a beginning diagnostic understanding. (This understanding was facilitated by the patient's having filled out before the initial meeting a self-administered test procedure, which included semiprojective questions, her family constellation, and other life data [Appelbaum 1973b]. A full battery of individual tests would likely have been even more useful.) I worked in accordance with what Malan (1963) recommended on the basis of his findings. I offered interpretations not only earlier but somewhat more directly than I would have if the treatment had been undertaken without a stipulation as to the small number of hours. I used the understanding of personality provided by psychoanalysis. The patient and I tied relationships from the past to the present, especially from mother to husband and to myself. We worked with the idealization that might have remained if the negative aspects of the transference had not been discussed, especially her anger over termination, a task held by Malan (1963) to be necessary for a good result. There is nothing in brief psychotherapy or in using Parkinson's Law that in principle need contradict the essentials of psychoanalytic understanding. The basic tenets of the method and means of understanding remain, while allowing a range of technical decisions (Ramzy 1961).

To those who consider psychotherapy a science in which observations are made of as large a field as possible with the least amount of observer influence on it, the Parkinson approach would smack of therapeutic rather than scientific zeal, in that it would influence and diminish the field of observation. The unconscious is endless, however, and observations are always limited arbitrarily by termination. The *lack* of a specified ending also deletes something from the field of observation, namely, the patient's reactions to an experience whose precise end is known in advance from the beginning. Rather than simply introducing a limiting variable by setting the end at the beginning, one limit is exchanged for another.

How long a treatment would be responsive to Parkinson's Law? For some patients and some therapists there may be varying temporal points beyond which setting the end at the beginning would be irrelevant, harmful, or beneficial. These are empirical and answerable questions. Invoking Parkinson's Law would seem most useful and appropriate for short-term psychotherapy. Over a short period of time, it could be expected to be best kept in mind and thus to be most effective and would likely have the least damaging transference implications.

As noted by Mann (1973) and experienced by me, the countertransference implications also are substantial. In addition to the general fear of innovation, short-term psychotherapy with the time limit set at the beginning inclines one toward a fear of having cheated the patient of the time he needs. Complaints by patients that they still are miserable and need more time are especially difficult to bear and to analyze when the patients have had, in reality, a treatment that is brief in comparison with many of one's other patients. At such times the therapist may be inclined to fret that the gains may not last and that his reasons for going ahead and sticking with such a truncated schedule are suspect. Some of this is due to fantasy and fear, a result of the anxiety of separation which is shared by patient and therapist; some is due to the therapist's pride, conscientiousness, and sense of professional responsibility. Pragmatically, these feelings are resolved most easily by selecting for such treatments only those patients who for financial or other reasons cannot have or will not agree to long-term psychotherapy.

Most people who undergo both kinds of treatment probably

agree that the gains from long-term psychotherapy are more extensive and durable. All other things being equal, I would recommend extended treatment. But all things usually are not equal. Individual differences within the patient require that we guard against the twin dangers of recommending long-term psychotherapy to practically everybody who presents himself with a psychiatric problem and of convincing ourselves that everybody can be helped by the kind of brief psychotherapy described here.

Suppose, in two years, the ex-schoolteacher was doing much worse than when I last saw her? This could be taken as evidence that the nine hours either had no effect on her or was harmful, giving her a little unresolved insight that if anything, made her sadder and more anxious and in greater conflict than she had been before. Such a line of reasoning depends, however, on the belief that all patients maintain their gains after having been treated by long-term psychotherapy. Test results from the Psychotherapy Research Project of the Menninger Foundation (Appelbaum 1977a) contradict this assumption. One-quarter of the patients considered at termination to have improved had taken a turn for the worse by the time they were examined two years later at follow-up. As far as I know, comparable figures for similar patients treated with brief psychotherapy are not available. I believe that the aforementioned patient would have made more gains with more time. But I do not know of any formal research that would support this, especially on whether such added gains would be commensurate with the time added in long-term psychotherapy. Reports by Malan (1963), Mann (1973), and Balint et al. (1972) do suggest that stable and substantial gains can be realized through brief treatment. At the least, gains from brief psychotherapy with the time limit set at the beginning should outstrip what might be expected on the basis of a similar time segment undertaken without the benefit of the effects of Parkinson's Law.

Brief psychotherapy, then, can be seen as a microcosm of the effects of the more general situation of working in psychotherapy with an end in sight. That situation provides moments rich with the possibilities of beneficial psychotherapeutic change.

Part II

Catalysts of Change: Evocativeness and Psychological-Mindedness

Perhaps because of their medical context, both psychotherapy and psychotherapists are often assumed to be homogeneous: Psychotherapy is compared to a medicine, doses of which are identical. Psychotherapists are chosen for clinical or research purposes as if all psychotherapists were the same and could be expected to purvey a standard medicine in a standard manner with more or less standard results. The facts are different. Psychotherapy is intensely personal, and its course is tied directly to the nature of the persons involved. Thus patients can be distributed according to how amenable they are to a particular variety of psychotherapy and to a particular psychotherapist. Such a distribution is based primarily upon intrapsychic factors and to a lesser extent upon external factors. Psychotherapists can be distributed according to how generally effective they are with particular kinds of patients. This distribution also is determined by intrapsychic factors, in addition to differences in training and theoretical orientation. In this section I shall discuss separately two intrapsychic factors that I believe contribute much to the nature and efficiency of psychotherapy. Though each one is discussed mostly in reference to its relative presence or absence in the therapist or patient, in fact each affects both participants in the psychotherapeutic process.

6

Change through Evocativeness

"It is not alone that the 'voice of the intellect is soft;' it speaks with two voices" (Richfield 1954, p. 407).

Freud's remarks on free-floating awareness, later known as "listening with the third ear," initiated a technique by which the psychoanalytic therapist learns the hidden connotations of a patient's words. The therapist might profitably also attend to the connotations of his own behavior. For in addition to what he means to convey, the evocativeness of how he conveys it may add to or detract from his therapeutic effectiveness. Just as the therapist listens with a third ear, he speaks with a second voice.

"Evoke" means, according to Webster's unabridged dictionary, "to call out; to summon forth, as from seclusion or the grave." Its etymological root is *vox* or voice. For much of the time the therapist attempts to summon forth, as from seclusion, feelings, buried memories, images, and ego states. He does this, not exclusively but to a great extent, with the voice. If "to evoke" is a task of the therapist, then it would seem that to be evocative, or evocativeness, is relevant to a full understanding of the effectiveness of psychoanalytic treatment and a way of accounting for the effectiveness of any particular therapist. Although this is not a new idea, it is too often overlooked or underemphasized. This is perhaps at least one reason for the recent proliferation of explicitly humanistic and existential schools that claim that psychoanalysis, through its preoccupation with concepts of structure, dynamics, and energy, overlooks the richness of human experience. In this chapter I shall explain "evocativeness" as a relevant variable in producing change in psychotherapy, calling attention to its connections with the theory of insight and with aspects of the psychotherapeutic interaction. In so doing, I shall compare psychoanalytic psychotherapy and art and suggest that evocativeness in therapy is similar to that in art.

In its earliest days, psychoanalysis was considered to be a simplistic information theory. By decoding the sender, Freud, as the receiver, learned the "sense" of what had been a jumble. Then he became the sender who told the patient the discovered meanings by means of interpretations. Freud then observed that though many of these interpretations were "right," change would most likely occur if he could release the affect attached to the heretofore misunderstood, or forgotten, event or fantasy. By recognizing the limitations of this formulation and spurred by further observation, the theory of technique moved on to include the concept of resistance, which led to the understanding and analysis of character and to the recognition and use of the transference, which in turn led to advances in knowledge of the unconscious and the curative results of recreating not only repressed single events but also repetitive trends.

The theory and specification of relations between affect and insight and the relationship between the two of them and change were put aside. As Richfield (1954) explained, "How any cognition is related to its alleged component in 'emotional insight' has not been satisfactorily stated. Generally, the contrast merely signifies a vague difference between an intellectual understanding and some kind of understanding accompanied by an emotional reaction" (p. 394). Reid and Finesinger (1952) noted that an emotional response is released or set off by an insight that itself need not be about an emotion. In other words, insights or cognitions can vary in emotional quality quite apart from whether they refer to something laden with emotion. "What is needed," Richfield (1954) added, "is some account of how any insight, an essentially cognitive process, can manifest the emotive properties necessary to effect the behavioral readaptations involved in cure" (p. 399).

One reason for the unsolved problem of the relations between intellect and emotion in the clinical process may be their dichotomization, for conceptual and heuristic reasons. The data of psychoanalysis are unitary. One can know a fact if the object of the knowing is factual; one can "know" an emotion if the object of the "knowing" is emotional. But knowing psychoanalytic data is neither solely factual nor solely emotional. Every mental content, idea, or feeling has its substrate in drive, as Rapaport (1950) discovered. The therapist, in practice, does not simply teach an idea, encourage a feeling, enable the patient to enliven an idea with feeling or to subject a feeling to control with an idea. What the therapist does is to help the patient to have in the present, through transference or recall, experiences with roots in his past, which are ordinarily unavailable to him in the present. Having a new experience, or having an old experience in a new way, includes the elements of feeling, thinking, and perceiving. Kohut (1959) approached the problem of recognizing conceptual frames of reference as distinct from the working data of treatment by showing that the one and only source of psychoanalytic data is subjective impression. Facts, such as those gathered by psychiatric case history, psychological examination, or social work, may or may not be related to the essence of the matter which is how things seem from moment to moment to patient and therapist.

The dichotomy between fact and emotion, as applied to insight, was discussed by Richfield (1954) who, quoting Bertrand Russell, distinguished between knowledge by *description* and knowledge by *acquaintance*. The latter is how most people know the effects of alcohol, i.e., experientially; the former is how most people know the effects of morphine, only through facts about it, or indirectly, through analogy or inference. For a curative integration to take place, knowledge by description — a level removed from the patient's experience — requires change to knowledge by acquaintance. Proceeding from Freud's aphorism about the problem of cure in psychoanalysis, that one cannot overcome an enemy who is absent, Richfield (1954) wrote:

> When our insights are knowledge by description, we have truths about the repressed enemy, not the enemy itself. The latter is known directly only when brought through the psychological barriers of the mind. Our insight is then knowledge by acquaintance. . . . (p. 403)

> Only when knowledge takes this form is it possible for the cognitive object to receive the necessary integration into the ego. The conscious personality cannot learn to handle a need of which it is unaware. But the awareness must have the need itself as its object, and not merely facts about it, before change in the distribution of cathexes are to be brought about. (p. 402)

As Kris (1950) asserted, "the full investment by the ego, the syntonicity of the event with superego and id strivings may then lead to the feeling of certainty, to the change from 'I know of' to 'I believe'" (p. 548). Eissler (1965) offered two criteria of knowledge from the psychoanalytic point of view.

> [(1) It] must not be isolated from the subject's previous knowledge, but must be in maximum associative connection with all systems of the personality . . . all of the implications inherent in an intellectual context must come to the subject's awareness. (2) Knowledge . . . is evaluated primarily in terms of the emotional reverberations of the particular content. Indifference to knowledge is tantamount to the absence of knowledge. (p. 67)

In explaining why symptoms persist even after resistances are surmounted and when both analyst and patient know the unconscious trend, Strachey (1934) stated, that it becomes evident that there were two senses in which a patient could become conscious of an unconscious trend; he could be made aware of it by the analyst in some intellectual sense without becoming "really" conscious of it. . . . A mutative interpretation [one that brings about change, as contrasted with interpretations in the sense of mere translation] can only be applied to an id-impulse which is actually in a state of cathexis. Every mutative interpretation must be emotionally "immediate"; the patient must experience it as something actual. (p. 23)

This is why the transference interpretation, Strachey (1934) continued, is most likely to be effective. "Instead of having to deal as best we may with conflicts of the remote past, which are concerned with dead circumstances and mummified personalities, and whose outcome is already determined, we find ourselves in an actual and immediate situation in which we and the patient are the principal characters" (p. 132).

Both kinds of knowledge are required for optimal therapeutic effectiveness: "the repressed drives of the patient [must] be known by acquaintance, and the significant facts pertaining to these drives, which psychodynamic theory enables us to discover, [must] be understood through the descriptive insights ultimately gained by therapy" (Richfield 1954, p. 405).

Art is another discipline that has as its objective the production of an effect through multi-layered communication. A comparison of objectives, processes, and techniques of psychoanalytic psychotherapy and art will contribute a richer context for evocativeness and will help clarify the artistic aspects of psychotherapeutic technique.

Similarities between psychoanalysis and art were specified by Kris (1952), Milner (1952), Beres (1957), and Schafer (1959), and these writers should be credited for much of what follows.

Addressing the same issues but writing in the context of language and art, Cassirer (1946) demonstrated the need to recover "the . . . wealth and fullness of immediate experience" and of primary mythological thinking through art. Art is "one

intellectual realm in which the word not only preserves its original creative power, but is ever renewing it . . . this regeneration
is achieved as language becomes an avenue of artistic expression. Here it recovers the fullness of life; but it is no longer a life
mythically bound and fettered, but an aesthetically liberated
life" (p. 98). Kris (1952) speculated that one reason for the bard
in primitive society, and fiction and drama in ours, was to find a
way for fantasies to be expressed outside the strictures of the
superego. Tarachow (1965) pointed out that the relief from the
burdens of such ego functions as synthesis and fusion of ambiv-
alent tendencies can be gained through art as through psychoanalysis. "There are only two types of education which help us
preserve our childish qualities without shame. These are
psychoanalytic education and artistic education" (p. 99). He
showed that art, like wit, enlarges our associative powers,
expressing impulses in socially acceptable, ego-controlled ways.
Low (1935) used a similar model by applying Freud's description
(1908) of the artist to the psychoanalyst:

> The artist (for artist we may here substitute analyst) . . .
> in contact with the external world (for which we may sub-
> stitute patient) obtains his material, molds and illuminates
> it by fusion with his own unconscious, and presents it
> again, thus re-shaped in forms acceptable to reality demands
> and to the unconscious of the world (the patient). (p. 8)

These authors seem to agree as to the teleology of psychoanalysis and art. Functions of the two, as applied to the individual "audience" or patient to secure immediate objectives, are
similar as well. The objective of art—that which distinguishes
art from mere entertainment—is to enable man to transcend
himself, to become even briefly something he ordinarily is not,
ultimately something above himself. Each man has his special
repertoire of ego states. What he "ordinarily is" refers to those
few ego states that are customary for him. What he "ordinarily
is not" refers to those extraordinary experiences that are relatively inaccessible because of being unconscious or because of
their poor fit with the organization of his repertoire. For

example, a mild man may be quite unaware that he wishes for the swashbuckling role. Or he may be aware of this potentiality within him but is unable to exploit it because it would feel awkward and alien in his workaday world. To be "above himself" is to deploy drives aimed at gratification in ways not harmless to society but instead integrative, communicative, and even inspiring. This is usually called sublimation.

A person walking the street in a state of mind of daily familiarity is relatively insusceptible to experiences markedly different from his usual ones. But as he waits expectantly for the curtain to go up or the symphony to begin and examines the title page or enters the art museum, he suspends his usual disbelief and is open to a new sense of participation in life, a new sense of self. So, too, it is with a person who decides to get help with his life. He is now, by definition, open to the quest for a new sense of self. Both audience and patient then embark on a course that is in persistent danger. Both may take it all in but miss the point entirely. Both may be tempted to leave. Both may pick and choose only what they are persuaded or moved by. Both the therapist and the artist know that they must employ the greatest skill in order to maintain and enhance the delicate process of involvement. Both of them strive to re-create the old — repressed ego states, identities, imagoes, ways of thinking, feeling, and behaving. Both offer the new, as synthesized from the reexperiencing of the ordinarily unavailable past with the mature equipment of the present. Both require tempering the emotions with control, form, and order. Both may relieve the exposition from time to time with humor, diversion, or other means of support. Both deal with fundamental issues and needs of life. Although the artist is ordinarily satisfied to secure his objectives temporarily, there may be those among the artistic audience whose whole lives are enriched by artistic experience. Although the therapist ordinarily hopes to enrich the whole life of his patient through the therapeutic experience, there are those who benefit from it only temporarily. Low (1935) suggested that the effect from this work on both artist and analyst is release. Supporting this are the observations that both are willing to undergo long training, both often experience a kind of fulfillment in their work, and many members of both pursuits probably would continue it even if it had no pecuniary and social rewards.

This conceptualization of the process between therapist and patient and between artist and audience is indebted to the work of Schafer (1959) from the standpoint of empathy and to Beres (1957) for his analogy between artist and analyst. Both these writers, in turn, have acknowledged their indebtedness to Kris (1952).

The process between artist-audience and therapist-patient affords an opportunity for both partners — not just the artist and the therapist — to share at least some of what may be considered art. The patient as an artist attempts to tell the therapist-audience about his experiences. The patient may be a poor artist or no artist at all, his communications serving merely to transmit facts. Or he may, and if all goes well increasingly does, not only transmit facts but also relive his recollections and reports. In so doing he is mastering the task of the poet as expressed by A. E. Houseman (1933): "And I think that to transfuse emotions — not to transmit thought but to set up in the reader's sense a vibration corresponding to what was felt by the writer — is the peculiar function of poetry" (p. 8). The patient as artist meets the artistic challenge by becoming increasingly tolerant of impulses, by his relative tolerance for primary process, and by the lifting of repressions, along with other hallmarks of regression. If the regression is controlled and goal oriented, it is a regression in the service of the ego, one in a series of normal regressions such as sleep, dreaming, wit, and orgasm, as well as creative activity (Kris 1952).

The judgment of whether or not a communication is art is that made by the subjective reaction of the special kind of receiver that we call the audience. (Whether the judgment is valid depends on the sophistication of any particular audience. As in science, a work is more or less "scientific" if it is recognized as such by the scientific community.) Art is not only influenced by the audience, it is also defined by the audience. The artist who ignores this, through narcissism or lack of talent, is ignored in turn. The painter Marcel Duchamp (Tompkins 1965) described the artist as

> a "mediumistic being" who does not really know what he is doing or why he is doing it; it is the spectator who, through a kind of "aesthetic osmosis," deciphers and interprets the work's hidden qualities, relates them to the external world, and thus completes the creative cycle. The spectator's contribution is consequently equal in importance to the artist's and perhaps even greater in the long run. (p. 37)

The psychoanalytic analogue of the influence of audience (the therapist) on artist (the patient) is found in the truism that whatever the patient does in the hour, even what he dreams outside the hour, has some reference to the analyst.

Just as there are good artists, there are good audiences. What Reik (1948) called the psychoanalytic response — the reaction of the analyst to the communications, words, gestures, pauses, and so forth of the analyzed person — is the product of an intuitive, empathic decoding process labeled "listening with the third ear." It, too, is an act of creation, dependent on the same controlled, regressive process as is utilized in artistic productivity. This kind of creativity — to experience faithfully in oneself the manifest and latent, primary and secondary, conscious and unconscious, past and present, direct and symbolic, and specific and allusive dimensions of another's experience — may be conceived as the passive aspect of the artistic process. For the conventional artistic audience, the process stops at this point. For the "artist" as practitioner, the process goes on to its active, productive aspect. The artist, for whom the outer world has been a stimulus to his largely infantile and unconscious creative self, becomes a stimulus to the outer world (now his audience) through his product. The therapist, for whom the patient has been a stimulus to his largely infantile and unconscious creative self, now becomes a stimulus to the outer world (the patient) through his therapeutic interventions.

In principle, the active, productive aspect would seem to be the reverse of the same process as the passive, receptive one, presumably with a better repertoire of technical devices available to the therapist or artist. In addition to aiding integration by the ego on the basis of knowledge by description, the therapist has the tasks of re-creating the fullest, richest experience of the past in the present and of enlarging the awareness of the present; in short, of encouraging knowledge by acquaintance. In this evocative aspect of his work, the therapist takes on the task of the poet. As a psychoanalyst (Beres 1957) described it, he is "to bring to the surface emotions and images (which are id derivatives)" (p. 419); and as a musician (Szigeti 1963) expressed it, not to "translate or interpret [but to make] music live" (p. 304). He seeks to avoid the situation with the patient that Hamlet seems to protest in the following: "You would seem to know my steps and you would pluck out the heart of my mystery; you would sound me from my lowest note to the top of my compass, and there is excellent service in this little organ; yet cannot you make it speak" (Shakespeare, lines 367–371). In his evocative task, the therapist exercises what Wordsworth (Grossart 1876), declared is characteristic of the poet, that is, a greater power to express thoughts and feelings produced in him.

Wordsworth's remark is systematized and extended by Freud (1908) in "Creative Writers and Day-dreaming." Here Freud proposed that stimuli for creative productions, as for dreams, arise from unsatisfied infantile wishes that have been stirred by daily events. For the therapist, some of these events are the patient's productions. Accessibility to his own infantile experience makes possible his creative reception of the patient's experiences and contributes to his helping the patient become more in touch with the infantile aspects of his life.

As Loewenstein (1956), explained,

> In the peculiar dialogue going on between patient and analyst, their mutual understanding is based on the general property of human speech to create states of mind in the interlocutor akin to those expressed by the spoken words. The function of representation in speech elicits images and representations in the addressee which are similar to those

used by the addressor. The expressive function tends to arouse emotions or states similar to those expressed. (p. 465)

Certainly, speech is the major avenue of communication in psychotherapy. But by attending to the evocative functions of the therapist and artist, one is encouraged to recognize that communication includes all avenues of expressiveness—bodily movements (Birdwhistell 1959), linguistics (Pittenger 1960, McQuown 1957, Rousey and Moriarity 1965), language itself as a transmitter of layered meanings (Lowenstein 1956), and as a construction of layered meanings (Thass-Thienemann 1963). Seen this way, therapist-patient communication is brought into line with the general definition of communication as "all the procedures by which one mind may affect the other . . . not only written and oral speech, but also music, the pictoral arts, the theatre, the ballet" (Shannon and Weaver 1949, p. 3). As Ruesch (1961) expressed it,

Language forces us to dissect in order to talk, and only if one who reads or hears words puts them together again can he hope to get an idea of what the other one is talking or writing about. It is the task of the therapist to choose words and gestures which, when combined within the head of the patient, will produce something that is alive. Unlike the scientific expert who chooses his words in such a way that the dictionary definition corresponds to the state of affairs to be described, the therapist cares for the impact words have upon people . . . [a task of the psychotherapist] is to produce an effect. (p. 30)

Evocativeness refers to one aspect of the production of an effect: it may be defined as how much a communication connotes. Although the therapist listens with his third ear to facilitate the connotations of the patient's communication, he speaks with the "second voice" of evocativeness to enhance the therapeutic aspect of his communication to the patient.

Evocativeness, like talent, is more easily recognized than explained. Both are subject to various analyses of their component parts. The artist may be judged as to his sense of rhythm, grace of body, or use of color. One approach to judging therapists was offered by Butler (1962). He classified therapists' productions according to Freshness of Words and Combinations ("the most highly connotative language possible seems to be poetic, metaphorical language in which much sensory imagery is used . . . the use of metaphor which adds vividness and color to the primary experience.") (p. 192); Voice Quality ("is he actually bringing something as a person, something that provides or generates new interpersonal experience for the client? is he simply 'present and accounted for'? or is he actually removing something from the situation through dullness, weakness, or through empty and forced attempts to be something which at that moment he isn't") (p. 192); and Functional Level of Responses ("how much are the therapist's remarks directed at the meaning or impact of experience?") (p. 193). Butler's classification is in some respects an extension of Sharpe's position (1951) that the language of clinical psychoanalysis is closer to poetry than to science. The total situation, too, may be assessed for its contribution to evocativeness. Thus, in the production of a play, besides the script, there are the contributions of acting, directing, scenery, costumes, make-up, and expectations aroused by publicity. The effect of therapy, at least until analyzed in the treatment, cannot avoid being influenced by the social esteem in which it is held, the prestige and background of the therapist as these may be known to the patient, the means of referral, and the physical accommodations.

Some questions for research are the extent to which evocativeness may be an unvarying attribute or an epiphenomenon of a particular therapist-patient dyad. What would be evocative to one patient might be inhibitory to another. Evocativeness in any one psychotherapeutic situation may be entirely a function of empathy with, and understanding of, a particular patient. Thus, the therapist might be evocative with some patients and not others or evocative in different ways with different patients.

An atomistic view of evocativeness would specify its relationship with personality variables such as control and intensity of affects and anxiety, content and formal characteristics of fantasy, and styles of delay between thought and action.

To what extent is a therapist evocative in therapy alone or in other situations as well? The voice and manner of some therapists change during the psychoanalytic hour from what they are in more ordinary interaction. Are such changes relatively conscious and calculated? Or are they artifacts of a smoothly functioning "regression" in order to put evocativeness at the service of the ego? Those whose style in this respect remains the same in or outside the therapeutic hour may be people who are naturally evocative. Or they may be people who cannot alter their natural expressive style in order to become optimally evocative.

What is the relationship between creative listening and creative speaking, the "third ear" and the "second voice"? Presumably there would be at least these alternatives: (i) a therapist who listens primarily in an intellectual, noncreative way and responds in the same way; (ii) a therapist who listens creatively and responds evocatively; (iii) a therapist who listens creatively but responds mechanically; and (iv) a therapist who listens mechanically but responds evocatively. (That is, he could, as some actors can do even with pallid material, make evocative even "wrong" or irrelevant content.)

Evocativeness has been discussed here mainly with reference to expressive therapeutic work. One may ask whether it is important elsewhere in the repertoire of expectable therapeutic situations. There are times, for example, when the therapist may feel called upon to evoke or sharpen in the patient's mind a particular image of himself, rather than working evocatively with the patient's own material. For instance, when a patient is overwrought and disorganized, the therapist may, for supportive reasons, wish to set a tone of coolness and deliberation and renewed or increased confidence in himself and the therapeutic process. Besides those situations in which it is advisable for the "realness" of an object to be evoked, one may consider that the whole therapeutic process is, in a sense, dependent upon the therapist as a real object (Loewald 1960). This real therapeutic object is one of integrity, dependability, and compassion. The emergence and maintenance of such an object, in alliance with the patient, makes it possible for the patient to talk freely and persist despite discouragement and fear. The establishment of such an object by the therapist is not a function of role playing or histrionics; but it does require a kind of self portrayal, particularly with those patients or at those times when the patient's expectations of people are quite different.

In much research on therapy, therapists are treated as interchangeable elements, or else there is an attempt to make them equal with regard to training and theoretical background. If individual differences in evocativeness have a substantial influence on any aspect of the therapeutic process or result, then the notoriously equivocal and negative results of such research may be explained (at least in part) by referring to this uncontrolled variable. Eissler (1965) believed that "a synthesis of knowledge with its corresponding emotions is one of the most difficult and delicate of tasks, that it is because of their failure to complete it that a good many analyses come to naught" (p. 67). The lack of control over the variable of evocativeness would help explain the imperfect correlation between the training of the therapist and his results, and between therapists of the same training and other evidences of individual differences. In the continued informal research of which every therapy consists — observation, formation of hypotheses, and checking of hypotheses — it could help account for the failure of theoretically well conceived hypotheses, as well as for the success of ones that are theoretically "wrong."

The suggested variable of evocativeness is in the tradition of phenomenology, humanism, and subjectivity. It may seem at first to be tangential or even to conflict with topographical, economic, and structural approaches. Rather, the apparent differences stem from differing levels of discourse rather than substance. The emphasis on evocativeness is complementary to any psychoanalytic approach. In its inductive crucible psychoanalysis is the communication of human experience.

7

Change through Psychological-Mindedness

The essence of psychoanalytic change is the patient's discovery of the psychological meanings of his behavior. Yet a major aspect of this work, his psychological-mindedness, has been at times ignored, at other times reified, and has remained generally undelineated and unsurveyed. Indeed, even the assertion that there is such an ability plunges us into a thicket of ambiguous issues. Is there one ability or several related abilities? Are we talking about a capacity or an actuality? Is psychological-mindedness constitutional or acquired, independent of conflict or a function of conflict, culturally or nosologically influenced? How is it different from, for example, insight or introspection? These are some of the questions that will be posed here, in the hopes of providing a systematic context for future thought.

PRESENT STATUS AND HISTORY

Different people mean different things by "psychological-mindedness." Such words as insightfulness, reflectiveness, introspectiveness, capacities for self-observation, self-appraisal, and self-awareness are often used synonymously. The term "psychological-mindedness" is commonly used by those trained

111

or practicing at the Menninger Foundation. It was one of the "patient variables" of the Psychotherapy Research Project of the Menninger Foundation, whose longevity and numbers of publications have helped propagate it locally and elsewhere where the traditions of Menninger Foundation practice have taken hold. The term as such does not appear in *A Glossary of Psychoanalytic Terms and Concepts* (Moore and Fine 1968) or in the classical psychoanalytic writings. Such abilities or functions as might be considered psychological-mindedness, by whatever name, are discussed in the old literature under "indications for psychoanalysis." In keeping with the criticism that diagnosis is the weakest aspect of psychoanalytic thinking, usually only gross criteria, especially in the old literature, are offered there.

In "On Psychotherapy" Freud (1905) mentioned as indications for analysis education, fairly reliable character, normal mental condition (meaning not psychotic or confused), and age, a list that he reaffirmed in 1913 in "Further Recommendations in the Technique of Psychoanalysis." And even in 1937, in "Analysis Terminable and Interminable," he put the responsibility for success in analysis on three factors: strength of instinct, severity of early trauma, and "ego modifications," the last meaning the degree of or propensity for psychosis. Fenichel's indications (1945) for psychoanalysis are cast in nosological terms, and among his contraindications he includes age, feeble-mindedness, unfavorable life situations, triviality of neurosis, urgency of neurotic symptoms, severe disturbance of speech, and a lack of a reasonable and cooperative ego. The last, too, is cast largely in nosological terms, schizophrenics being unable to bring such an ego to the process, psychopaths being unwilling to do so, and "stubborn" people simply refusing to cooperate. Waldhorn (1960) characterized Glover's approach as follows: "His fundamental attitude remains, however, that the degree of accessibility to analysis is more or less the same for all cases within a diagnostic category" (p. 486).

One may argue that the classical explorers had some variations or elements of psychological-mindedness in mind, and that is probably true. But there is reason to consider whether there were substantive theoretical reasons for their extensive mention of it. The early view of psychoanalysis, still recognized as true though incomplete, is that if one can remove resistances, forgotten memories will be recovered, insights based on these will develop, and change will result. (As a consequence of this, there may still be some analysts who take the request for an analysis, or the bringing of symptoms, as sufficient indication for the patient's being put on the couch.) Implicit in this line of reasoning is the assumption that in relevant respects all people are much the same so that a standard technique should bring about a standard result. However, Freud's experiments with end setting, Ferenczi's "active technique," Alexander's and French's corrective emotional experience, and Eissler's parameters all illustrated the felt needs for psychoanalytic technique to change with respect to different people and different kinds of technical problems. This movement toward individual differences received great impetus with the shift from id to ego, Freud's structural theory, Anna Freud's analysis of the defensive function of the ego, and Hartmann's autonomous ego functions — in short, the development of ego psychology. This emphasis resulted in the somewhat reified ego of the older theory being analyzed into more or less separate functions or part-processes. A natural outgrowth of this is to consider in their own right those functions relevant to prescribing and carrying out psychoanalysis, among which is psychological-mindedness.

Psychological-mindedness as an explicit term does appear in two recent major statements on indications for analysis (Waldhorn 1967, p. 33; Namnum 1968, p. 271).

DEFINITION

The following definition of psychological-mindedness and sketch of its underlying characteristics are offered in the hope that they can lead to general agreement on linguistic usage and practical application: *"A person's ability to see relationships among thoughts, feelings, and actions, with the goal of learning the meanings and causes of his experiences and behavior."* This definition has four parts, the presence or absence of each of which may characterize a particular person, pose a particular technical problem, and result in a particular prognosis. (1) *The ability to see relationships and to learn meanings and causes.* (*a*) Cognition. This is central to the definition offered by Wallerstein and Robbins (1956) for use in the Psychotherapy Research Project of the Menninger Foundation, and it is explicit or implicit in other definitions and in common clinical usage. As a kind of basic science for psychological thinking, its at least minimal presence is a necessity no matter how well endowed a person might be in the other components of psychological-mindedness. Thus mental defectives, excessively literal obsessionals, and many organically damaged people, for example, tend to be unpsychologically minded. (*b*) Intuition and empathy. These complicated and ambiguous terms refer to the easily observed talent that some people have, and others lack, to "see," "know," and "feel" covert and inexplicit psychological events. (2) *The goal of learning the meanings and causes of . . . behavior.* A person may have the requisite cognitive abilities and intuitive talents but not have the *goal* of using them to learn psychological meanings or causes. To satisfy this requirement for psychological-mindedness, a person would have to have an interest in people as complex and motivated and to be intrigued by human nature. Those inclined this way wonder what makes people tick, why they say "ouch" and why they care so much about playing the piano. Human beings are, to them, more than muscular systems, more than socioeconomic-political roles. Rather they are life histories, caught at one point in time, many selves as well as one self, and capable of fine shades of experience that may be difficult to express. Such people have the capacity to survey life's horizons as well as its immediacies and to recognize their time as finite and their place as tiny in the shadows of infinity and humanity. Such a point of view, wedded to objectivity, results in a sense of the tragic. In turn the tragic sense escapes morbidity and resulting paralysis through the perspectives of irony and humor. (Humor also reflects capacities taking distance and finding adaptive expression of impulse, which are aspects of psychological thinking.) In Schafer's view (1970) an implicit recognition of tragedy and irony influences the selection of analytic patients and is "sometimes subsumed under psychological-mindedness" (p. 292).

If a person can be interested in himself and others in humanistic terms, then he is likely to be capable of the concern, regard, and object-commitment that distinguishes the use of psychological-mindedness for genuine and constructive purposes from its use as "pseudo-insight" (Kris 1956, Moore and Fine 1968) and for such uses as play, cleverness, or self-condemnation (such as Freud noted in his wry question about why people had to be depressed in order to see themselves so clearly (1917, p. 246)). The kind of interest in people described here, by definition, includes the maintenance of connections between affects and insight, for one could hardly explore people in this way without considering the emotional importance of events. As Fiedler (1968) explained it, "Without passion there *is* no truth." Psychology without affects may be appropriate for some kinds of study and research, but it is a contradiction in terms when the context is such that "psychology" refers to the truth about oneself and life. (Loewenstein (1967) suggested that the term "psychological grasp" should be used instead of "psychological-mindedness" in order to differentiate between intellectualized and pseudoscientific activities that serve resistance and genuine psychological-mindedness.) In summary, this definition of having the goal of relating oneself to a psychological understanding of human experience, refers to: (*a*) interest in the way minds work, (*b*) capacity for concern about self and others, and (*c*) ability to allow affects their rightful place. (3) *Causes of his experience.* The *direction* of a person's psychological thinking for purposes of treatment must be toward himself, in contrast to those who think psychologically only about other people or works of art. Self-directedness of psychological thinking is often expressed by such terms as self-observation, self-judgment, self-awareness, self-appraisal, and introspectiveness. (4) *Ability.* This is an estimate of a person's present and future ability to put his capacities for psychological thinking at the service of the psychoanalytic process. It is thus an operational concept. Judging such a concept requires a somewhat arbitrary criterion since every patient has resistances, and every analysis requires the establishment of a therapeutic alliance and of training in the ways of the process, as well as training in psychological thinking per se. Yet we do make decisions as to *the degree of* resistances, assets, and liabilities and as to the *likelihood* that psychological thinking can be made sufficiently available to the process to justify the beginning and continuation of treatment or the setting of particular goals. There is a point at which sufficient quantity allows, for operational and predictive purposes, asserting the presence or absence of a quality.

When, for brevity's sake, one declares a person to be or not to be psychologically minded, one is using these definitional characteristics as criteria: the person meets or does not meet these four criteria to a more or less arbitrary degree; or deficiencies in one or more are or are not compensated by excellence in others.

OTHER TERMINOLOGY

Probably the word most often used in connection with psychological-mindedness, and sometimes used to stand for it, is *insight*. Insight is defined in *A Glossary of Psychoanalytic Terms and Concepts* as "subjective experiential knowledge acquired during psychoanalysis of previously unconscious pathogenic content and conflict" (Moore and Fine 1968, p. 55). Thus insight comes about *as a result* of the process of discovery.

Useful semantic and conceptual clarity is gained by distinguishing between psychological-mindedness as a process and insight as the product of the process. This distinction tends to be muddied, however, especially when the term "insightfulness" is used, as occurs clinically and in the literature. Here, with the same root, the reference may not be to the fruits of the process but to the process or to the capacity to carry through the process.

This usage is often euphemistic or jargon. But it is the precise, technical usage in one of three definitions of insight available from the Psychotherapy Research Project of the Menninger Foundation. This one is on a list of definitions compiled by various project members where it is discussed as "a *process* through which a person attains self-awareness" (my italics).

Other project definitions raise other issues. Its first and central definition is in the description written by Wallerstein and Robbins (1956) of "patient variables": whether the patient sees his disturbed functioning as "maladaptive and as the proper object of therapy," the degree to which the discomfort is acknowledged as being an internal problem, and whether the patient is aware of some connection among "symptoms, behavior and underlying conflict." This definition refers only to one particular insight, expressed crudely as whether or not the patient knows he has a problem. It is a definition closely allied to motivation which may or may not be related to psychological-mindedness as defined here. The project's third definition of insight, by Rosen and Siegal, occurs in a separate but related investigation on the basis of the psychological test battery alone: "A change in some aspect of the patient's functioning brought about through and related to some increase in self-awareness" (Appelbaum 1977a). This definition includes insight, as the *Psychoanalytic Glossary* defines it, plus the stipulation that the insights result in change. If this definition were followed, then we would have to have a way of referring to those insights that do not result in change. This raises the issue of the relationship between insight and change. Are insights that do not result in change by definition the result of deficient psychological thinking, as defined here? Or is it possible that insight may develop according to our hypothesized characteristics but still not result in change?

I hope the sample citations of the various terms used to refer to psychological-mindedness support the need for agreement on one with specified referents, such as the definition suggested here.

These definitional issues are illustrated by the analysis of a married, middle-aged housewife and mother.

Let us apply the four parts of the definition of psychological-mindedness to Mrs A. (1) Though she was not to demonstrate the ability to see relationships or to be intuitive consistently or impressively for most of the analysis, Mrs A. did have such capacities. She showed them intermittently, usually with respect to people other than herself. They appeared almost by accident, often followed by a quick change of subject or other defensiveness. During the diagnostic examination, she achieved an IQ only slightly above average, but she gave various indications that her intellectual capacity was higher, with no obvious fundamental impairments of capacities for abstraction and memory; and she did show a potential for a greater amount and elaborateness of fantasy than she ordinarily displayed. (2) She indicated a basic regard and concern for people, as could be seen, for example, in her genuine desire and striving to be a good mother and community citizen. Although she could be vague and forgetful about many subjects, people as participants in her world were well defined (though her relationships with them were burdened by many self-defeating premises and conditions). However, she failed to give evidence of having the goal of thinking psychologically about herself. Indeed, she gave many indications of how important it was for her not to think that way. Even in the midst of the "depression," which was the reason she had been referred for treatment, she petulantly objected to the idea that what to her were perfectly innocent and straightforward situations could have meanings. "Does everything *have* to have a meaning?" she irritably asked the psychologist who was testing her. She was alert to the affective qualities of life events, but at the beginning and through much of the analysis the intensity and variety of feelings that she allowed herself were restricted subdued. Rather than showing wonder or excitement at a new psychological idea, she tended to react to it with the same monotonous voice that she ordinarily used in describing the day's mundane activities. At the same time, she recognized that she lived in fear of being overwhelmed by her feelings should she begin to allow their expression. (3) Especially as the analysis continued, Mrs A. showed much interest and some capacity for thinking psychologically about members of her family and her friends. But such interest and ability usually deserted her when the direction of psychological thinking was toward herself. (4) Mrs A. had failed Criteria 2 and 3 and could not, at the beginning of the analysis, be described as being psychologically minded. Her capacity to become so hinged to a large extent on those underlying attributes described below as structural and functional aspects of psychological-mindedness (capacities for ideation, anxiety tolerance, and the like), and thus an intensive diagnostic examination was required as part of the decision to attempt analysis. These underlying attributes seemed sufficient to result in mild encouragement about her prospects for analysis. Her extreme defensiveness whenever issues of symbolic meanings were raised suggested strongly that there were powerful dynamic forces working against psychological-mindedness. In principle these could be worked with to free her capacity. But at the same time the extent of her defensiveness suggested that it would be a long, difficult task. (It is unusual, for example, on psychological tests for otherwise inhibited patients openly to fight off suggestions of psychological meanings to test productions.) Environmental influences, to be described below, for the most part worked against her chances of becoming psychologically minded. But she did seem, even at the beginning, to realize that her whole life had for a long time been unsatisfactory to her and that her presenting complaints were merely symptomatic of this. In summary, though psychological-mindedness was not available at the beginning, there was a small but reasonable possibility that it could become so.

STRUCTURAL AND FUNCTIONAL ELEMENTS
OF PSYCHOLOGICAL-MINDEDNESS

To the degree that psychological-mindedness is dependent upon and defined by structural capabilities, one can understand that it is spoken of as if it were either present or absent. Structures are enduring, and we tend to think about the capacities based on them as being there or not there, as permanent characteristics. Musical talent, for example, can be encouraged, developed, and trained, but people nonetheless vary widely in their proficiency, even though given the same training opportunities. We are comfortable, at least with respect to extremes, in saying that they either have it or do not have it, based on the assessment of particular structures that make this talent possible, e.g., tonal memory, pitch discrimination, sense of meter and rhythm. Though structures relevent to psychological thinking are unlikely to be entirely absent in anybody, nonetheless their great quantitative differences do make for a qualitative "presence."

Terms from different levels of abstraction and from different theories are used to describe those structural attributes and functions relevant to psychological-mindedness. For example, the *Glossary* mentions: "Among the more important autonomous ego functions (involved in the coming about of insights) are self-observation, synthesis, perception, memory and reality testing, control of regression and affective discharge, and integration" (Moore and Fine 1968, p. 55). Throughout the literature there is a linguistic and conceptual ebb and flow among terms as used in academic psychology (memory, perception, abstraction), often adapted to and melded with psychiatric concepts (synthesis of parts of the personality, reality testing), and psychological concepts (capacity of the ego to split itself).

Since psychological-mindedness involves coming to consciousness and manipulating ideas, *ideational capacities* would seem a sine qua non. To what extent is the person's attention characteristically fastened to the objective givens of the "external" world as compared to subjective "inner" self-developed and elaborated ideas? Ideational capacities can be described in terms of quantity, complexity, speed of movement, and variety and richness of content. Closely correlated with these abilities is *verbal ability*, and indeed most of our ways of knowing about ideational and fantasy abilities are through verbal mediation. (Stone [1967, p. 42], however, warned against the possibility of verbal ability's being a superficial aspect of the patient's character, operating in the service of resistance or, as an [oral] pleasure-producing end in itself.) A further quality of ideation is the *capacity to think abstractly or concretely*, as the occasion may require. As an aid to psychological-mindedness this capacity is often termed simply the capacity for abstraction because abstraction is a later developed and more difficult form of mentation than concreteness, and it may be that most insights do proceed from the concrete to the abstract. However, we also require that the patient be able to think concretely, especially as we may emphasize the concrete aspects of his life in order to infuse the process with feeling and to avoid the use of abstraction as a defense. The *capacity for integration* lies at the heart of psychological thinking: the ability to pull together seemingly disparate ideas, events, and feelings so that their similarity can be noticed, and a new Gestalt or configuration, called insight, can be created. If this insight or configuration in turn helps bring together disparate parts of the personality, then, according to a distinction made by Kris (1956), a capacity for *synthesis* is enlisted as well.

Based on the initial examination, on isolated bits of evidence gathered during the early years of the analysis and on greater evidence at the end, Mrs A. had at least minimal capacities for abstraction, integration, and synthesis. She often created the impression of being tied to objective, day-to-day activities, which she herself described as trivia. But she was more ideational and introspective than that. She reported many dreams, spent much time in reverie, and regularly thought about the hour by herself, though she often created the impression during the hour that previous hours had simply vanished into the air.

Most of the functions mentioned can be considered as ego functions, but Loewenstein (1967) reminded us that psychological-mindedness is not only an ego function or a function of several ego functions. It "is undoubtedly influenced by factors from all psychic structures but particularly by the existence of a well-developed superego, since it is this structure which represents compliance with the injunction to be candid, to see, communicate, and think about all experience and behavior in the interest of cooperation with the analyst and the therapeutic intention" (pp. 44–45).

But it was just these injunctions with which Mrs A.'s superego could not allow compliance. She was in thrall to other, stronger, injunctions. For her it was dangerous to be offered the opportunity by the analytic situation to learn, know, and see. As indicated by her achieving an IQ much below her capacity, she had insulated herself from these felt dangers, complacent rather than humiliated at characterizing herself as "stupid." She claimed to be unable to understand anything about her husband's business or their finances. When it came out, usually inadvertently, that she was reading, she would maintain she could not remember the name of the author of a particular poem or book. When she took some college courses, she would learn the material but be unable to remember it for examinations. A plausible beginning to her taboo on "seeing" was her apparent repeated viewing of the primal scene. For many of her early years she and her parents slept in one bedroom. She occasionally had dreams of a screen behind which fearsome and exciting things were happening. She at first denied that she "knew any of this," despite the family's cramped bedroom arrangement, apparently content to leave unexplained how she possibly could not have seen her parents behaving sexually.

What did it mean to Mrs A. to be asked to "cooperate" with the analyst? Just as the patient was sexually responsive before and during the first week of marriage, she had an openly sexual dream about the analyst during the first week of the analysis. But sexual frigidity soon set in with her husband, and great inhibitions over such thoughts and feelings characterized most of the analysis. In short, the analysis quickly became erotized and then subject to her sexual taboos. An interpretation from the analyst was seen as an unwelcome intrusion into her. She symbolically refused entry into her vagina by keeping her legs rigidly crossed on the couch. The thoughts that she received "in her head," whether from the analyst or from herself, were viewed with the same blend of outward horror and inner enjoyment that she felt in response to directly sexual intrusions. She experienced interpretations as rapes, while through her lack of cooperativeness she created a countertransference situation in which the analyst had to "force" the insights into her. Covertly enjoying this, she could secretly accept insights, at the same time placating her superego by shifting the responsibility onto him. She could know about herself and others, peek into the mysteries of the dark, but not participate. To allow herself to enjoy the mutual task of bringing about insights would feel to her like having an affair with the analyst. As it was, the analytic meetings were to her all too much like an affair. The least she could do, according to her commands, was to refuse to cooperate.

Psychological thinking takes time, and the satisfactions from it are derivative as well as delayed, although the materials with which it works may be just those that press for immediate discharge. Thus it is understandable that psychological thinking requires *tolerance for frustration* and *tolerance for delay*.

Venturing into the unknown of thinking about oneself in new ways requires at least a minimal expectation that the unknown will become known and that one will find his way out of the unmapped territories of what had been unconscious. *Anxiety tolerance* is available on this basis and makes possible undertaking self-exploration, as well as other frightening situations of indeterminate outcome such as creative tasks in general. By the same token, when undertaking the re-creation of experience one must expect strong feelings, affects other than anxiety. Some people are overcome by affects when they think psychologically about themselves or are so afraid that they will be that they are unable to be psychologically minded. Thus psychological thinking is aided not only by the ability to experience affects and to integrate feelings with insights but also by the confidence in the capacity to control and modulate affects, by *affect tolerance.*

A rough, two-step model for psychological thinking would include: (1) A "passive-regressive" phase of allowing unconscious and preconscious ideas into consciousness, such as in free associations. The psychologically minded person must be able to negotiate this aspect of the basic rule as a necessary, but insufficent, condition. He must also be able to negotiate the next step. (2) The "active-progressive" phase of listening and trying to make new sense out of "what comes to mind." Though Step 2 is often only an implicit codicil to the basic rule, it is the most useful fulfillment of the basic rule.

This two-step model is similar to Kris's regression in the service of the ego (1952) which was considered applicable by him (1956) to psychological thinking: one of the functions of the ego in gaining psychoanalytic insight is "control of temporary and partial regression" (pp. 449–450). Erikson (1964) wrote: "Freud then discovered another principle . . . that *psychological discovery is accompanied by some irrational involvement of the observer, and that it cannot be communicated to another without a certain irrational involvement of both.*" Stone (1967) suggested that a patient can be analyzed only if he is incapable of shifting back and forth between fantasy and reality and between the past memories and associations and the present perception of reality.

The applicability of "regression in the service of the ego" to both art and psychological-mindedness alerts us to their comparability. Among a number of similarities, both art and psychological-mindedness emerge from a regressive-constructive process with something created anew. Both of their creations pertain to layers of meanings and textures of experience. And among the goals of each is a new view of life; it is more than coincidence that in both art and psychoanalysis one hopes to employ or achieve a sense of the tragic. Conceptualizing psychological-mindedness as a kind of artistic creativity has implications for the philosophy of psychoanalysis, for the selection and education of practitioners and patients and for technique.

With his stipulation of temporary and partial regression in the gaining of analytic insight, Kris (1956) added "the ability of the ego to view the self and to observe its own functions with some measure of objectivity . . ." (p. 450). Namnum (1968), too, cited "the capacity to take distance from one's emotional experience as a component of psychological-mindedness" (p. 271). In the process of psychological thinking, then, the ego is split between an observing part and an experiencing part — the observing part maintaining a relatively steady relationship with the objective part, while the experiencing part is allowed regressive shifts to bring new material for the integration that leads to insight.

As we have seen, Mrs A. had grave difficulties in allowing ideas into consciousness, a kind of passivity that was equated by her with sexual receptivity. "Activity" for her was equated with aggression and fell under equally strong taboos. A central determinant of her need to inhibit angry feelings was the death of one sister who suffered a birth injury and died when the patient was four. "Don't touch the baby," she remembered mother as saying, "Don't come near her or look at her." But the patient did these things and in a corner of her mind was glad the little competitor had died. Throughout her life the patient was preoccupied with the fear that her mother too would die. She repeatedly had images of her mother in a casket. Sometimes these occurred during sexual intercourse, which turned off any beginning sexual feelings.

With her father a ne'er-do-well and her mother felt as the only dependable source of security, the patient feared the loss of her one reliable parent should her mother learn of her anger, or should her anger be expressed in activity or assertiveness.

PLEASURE AS A MOTIVE FOR PSYCHOLOGICAL THINKING

Pleasure as a motive for psychological thinking is an extension of Criterion 2, the goal of psychological thinking as founded on interest and appreciation of the psychological side of human nature. Persons who find pleasure in psychological thinking approach the task sensing that the inherent rewards of the search, as well as the discovery, will be worth the effort. There is immanent gratification connected with the task, as the wish to know is combined with a wish to enjoy. Kuiper (1968) looked for prospective candidates for psychoanalysis among those who have "a very real pleasure 'in finding out' or discovering things about one's self . . ." (p. 263).

Zest in creating insight may be the same quasi-autonomous characteristic as zest in creating art and humor, a function of regression in the service of the ego and a sublimation. It may stem from the exercise and development of ego functions such as a child achieves in taking things apart and putting them back together, in exploring and in learning about the lawfulness of the world (White 1963).

The possible pleasures of creating an insight, especially should it come about through mutual participation with the therapist, were especially forbidden to Mrs A. It was unconsciously identical to her wish that her next youngest sister, the one who had died, had been a creation of hers and her father's. Her menstrual flow suddenly stopped for several weeks following a shared understanding that the meaning of it was to proclaim that she had not done anything forbidden with the therapist, that she had not created a baby-insight. Thus, rather than finding pleasure in creating insight, through much of the analysis the patient fled from what was to her a horror and fear of such creativity.

DYNAMIC INFLUENCES

As with any other skill or activity, psychological-mindedness can take on symbolic meanings that may facilitate or inhibit its functioning. To enumerate all such possible meanings would be to catalogue all human motivation. However, the nature of psychological thinking especially implicates such themes as looking and knowing, allowing entry into oneself, sharing an activity, and creating.

The above themes have already been mentioned with regard to Mrs A. Here we may add to this list and illustrate below Mrs A.'s resentment of felt demands upon her, her need to avoid besting her mother through succeeding in anything, to deprive the envied analyst of his assumed power, and to perpetuate the analysis in order to maintain sadomasochistic and oral-dependent satisfactions.

The patient had great difficulties having anything that her sisters and especially her mother, did not have, and this included the skill of psychological thinking. When mother visited her, the patient became the fool, dropping things, tripping over things, and not being able to operate household machinery. She lied about the size of her brassiere to her mother and sisters, so that they would not know that she "had more" than they did. When she got possessions that her mother and sister did not have, she hid them or felt very uncomfortable. This was one reason for her discomfort at having an analysis and one reason why she thought her mother should be in analysis too. But if Mrs A. alone had to have the analysis she could try to minimize her discomfort by cancelling its value.

Beneath Mrs A.'s submissiveness was a simmering fury against men. Partly out of her need to placate her mother, she too espoused her mother's view of women having to suffer the "curse," giving in to men's painful sexual demands, and remaining loyal to one man despite their opportunity to have other women. The patient first claimed to despise the sight of male genitals, but it turned out that she could less stand the sight of female ones. In her view women were worthless, and it was therefore understandable to her that as the first of several daughter "disappointments" to her father she was unwanted. To her the analyst had everything, and she had nothing. Thinking psychologically meant to her at times yielding to him. One way to avoid this, to deprive him of his felt power as an analyst, was through depriving herself of psychological thinking.

Especially when the patient was most flagrantly nonpsychologically minded, she would ask the analyst if he did not feel like beating her. Thus her lack of psychological-mindedness was one way she had of instituting and maintaining her infantile tie to her father, who did regularly beat her. Miserable as it was in some respects, this was the one kind of heterosexual relationship that she thought was available to her. While she maintained this relationship, she also maintained the security of the relationship with her mother, the daily visits from her now being joined by and later replaced by the daily visits of the analytic hour. To work psychologically with the analyst, detached from such object relationships, was for her to enter a great unknown, without much childhood precedent and experience to guide her. Finally, she knew that psychological-mindedness would be her means of bringing about the end of the analysis, one of the few great events in her self-denying life. Developing the capacity for psychological-mindedness and letting it be known that she was able to do this kind of work by herself meant to her to risk all.

DEFENSES AGAINST PSYCHOLOGICAL-MINDEDNESS

In principle, any defensive character pattern or mechanism can be enlisted against psychological-mindedness, since one function of all defenses is to narrow cognitive or emotional awareness, or both.

Mrs A. relied moderately on repression and little on intellectualization. More important to her were isolation of affect and relatively conscious withholding, avoidance, and denial. As these defenses weakened and insights were no longer described by her as meaningless or crazy, she would then employ externalization. "You think . . . ," she would say, or according to the cartoons and articles about psychoanalysis, such and such were true. At other times she drew herself up on a prudish high horse of morality, unwilling to soil herself with work on such dirty, bad ideas that had somehow gotten into mind. Or else she treated ideas as the currency of a socioeconomic exchange, to be apologized for, accepted as being taught to her in exchange for her fee, but not to be considered for the meanings she might extract and use from them.

NOSOLOGY, CULTURE, TREATMENT, AND DIAGNOSIS

A capacity for psychological thinking is roughly correlated with various major diagnostic groupings. It is less likely to be found among behavior disorders because of their characteristic low anxiety and frustration tolerances and oral-passive trends. The delay of impulse necessary for the experimentation with small quantities of impulse through thought and the self-help nature of psychological thinking are those very challenges that such people find so difficult to meet.

On the other hand, delay and self-help, along with capacities for abstraction and manipulation of ideas without the encroachment of anxiety and other affects, are the forte of obsessive-compulsive people. They tend, however, to employ these capacities for defensive purposes, failing in the affective component of psychological-mindedness.

Using experimental methods that delineate the cognitive principles of leveling and sharpening (Gardner et al. 1959), leveling has been shown to be related to repression (Holzman and Gardner 1960) and thus to hysteria. Such leveling works against the discovery, differentiation, and consequent mental manipulability of ideas and thus against psychological-mindedness.

Erotization of the analytic process, especially in the form of a wish-fear of the entry of ideas and feelings, poses special difficulties in some obsessive-compulsive and paranoid people, especially males, because of their fear of passive-receptiveness. For these people psychological thinking functions as a competitive defense, in which the goal is to top the analyst rather than to learn for oneself. In some sexual disturbances, especially among females, such erotization may lead to the uncritical, unintegrated acceptance of interpretations as gifts or thrills.

In the schizophrenias and other psychoses there may be too much "passive-regressive" psychological thinking and too much immediate knowing, without sufficient capacities for "active-progressive" integration. The associations follow too quickly and too far along drive-determined paths, without being able to establish new combinations of fewer drive-determined and more isolated and autonomous structures.

The notion that psychoanalysis is only applicable and useful to Western, middle-class people is often used to discredit its essential applicability to all humans. But this notion may carry a germ of truth. Certain cultures do seem more amenable to thinking in psychoanalytic terms than others. Zen Buddhists, as with other kinds of phenomenologists, encourage introspection and microscopic examination of experience as well as openness to affects. But they reject the hypothetical deductive manipulation of ideas and the creation of abstractions. Other religious and political philosophies answer psychological questions according to their own systems of thought; they tacitly or openly restrict the freedom to adopt psychological assumptions and to develop one's own conclusions. Note the biblical assertion that the thought equals the deed, with its implicit prohibitions against the wide-ranging freedom of thought necessary for psychological thinking. And note the Soviet hostility toward psychoanalysis in favor of political and economic explanations of behavior. Prominent American hypermasculine values of self-help and action are inimical to the sharing and introspectiveness of psychological thought in analysis. Freud (1926a), Menninger (1937), and Erikson (1951, p. 141) suggested a Jewish affinity for psychological thinking partly because of Jews' separateness from many nonpsychological, institutional ways of thinking and beliefs. Cultures that are faced with great environmental tasks or natural and human enemies may discourage the introspectiveness necessary for psychological-mindedness as being inimical to their need for single-mindedness and action. They may further discourage acknowledging the value of the individual in regard to the group, as is implied in psychoanalysis by so much time and money being expended upon one person. A good example of these trends is provided by Israel, where the natural pioneering tasks and the continued presence of external human enemies have instituted different mental health values while maintaining other similar Western traditions (Moses and Kligler 1966).

Mrs A.'s rural, poverty-stricken cultural beginnings were in many respects alien to the development of psychological-mindedness. With families large and death from disease common, it was every man for himself, or it was a loose federation of the group against the hostile environment. Demands for action were greater than demands for thought, and schooling was minimal and little valued. But "answers" were in abundance, founded upon fundamentalist religious values and concrete, traditional aphorisms, e.g., a man's nature is to drink and carouse with women; the stork brings babies; you must love every-one; and a nice girl does not have such thoughts. Mrs A. was much inclined to use such aphorisms as defenses against thinking indepen-dently, in addition to whatever stultifying effects they had upon her culturally. But she never really seemed to have fully entered into that culture. She recoiled from the chaos of impulsive action, and she espoused that local philosophy more out of fear than conviction. Although it was discouraged, she sometimes allowed herself to become a reader. With all the restrictions imposed upon it and with all the anxiety and guilt associated with it, thought became for her a refuge, a glass menagerie. These early experiences of separateness may have provided at least a weak precedent for allowing herself solitary, thoughtful moments, thus making it possible for her to be the one lonely member of her culture to have a psychoanalysis and, finally, to think about herself in psychological terms.

A relative lack of psychological-mindedness is one reason why some patients are offered psychotherapy rather than psychoanalysis. The increased direct participation of the ther-apist allows him to carry a greater share of the burden and thus to compensate for any particular weakness of the patient in this respect. To the extent that the psychotherapy is directed at one sector there is less need for integrative abilities. But following the belief that every psychotherapeutic treatment should be as expressive as possible, psychotherapy nonetheless does pose demands for psychological-mindedness. It does so even in those psychotherapies in which meeting the demands of psychological-mindedness as defined here is less the problem than are flagrant ruptures of the relationship, as in psychosis, and in the wholesale diversions of interest and attention, as in behavior disorders. Here the patient may use the psychotherapy to imitate or internalize helpful aspects of the therapist, benefiting from corrective emotional experiences and a generally benevolent interpersonal environment. It is easy, when speaking of or adopting this model, to sound as if psychological-mindedness has been at least for the moment, put aside. Yet how would one then differentiate this kind of psychotherapy from counseling and guidance? It is more likely that there is a kind of low-key, implicit psychological-mindedness at work even during such apparently nonpsychological problem-solving moments. It is only "as if" the requirements for psychological thinking had been put aside.

Mrs A. had been referred for psychoanalysis with the uneasy recognition that she was far from an ideal analysand, particularly because of her lack of psychological-mindedness. But her difficulties had so infiltrated and warped her character that psychotherapy could only have been expected to tide her over from one outbreak of symptoms to another, with life between symptoms being ungratifying. There were occasional episodes during the analysis, such as deaths in the family and declarations of leaving the analysis, when the analyst briefly had to use nonanalytic ways to ensure the continuation of the treatment. For the most part the patient allowed a stable field for psychological exploration. She did, however, mount a persistent and intense demand to shift the burden of psychological thinking from herself to the analyst. He had to supply the associations, put them together into a useful configuration of relationships, and take the responsibility for the "sin" that emerged. Thus, while maintaining the analytic structure, the patient attempted to turn analysis into psychotherapy.

Can a person be trained to become psychologically minded? Probably not, to the extent that it is dependent upon constitutional or other early developmental structures, just as high musical proficiency cannot be taught to those without basic musical abilities. But to the extent that it is interfered with by dynamic conflicts, the process of modulating and resolving conflicts should release the patient's potential capacity for psychological thinking. Something of a conundrum is implied here, since the process that is to release psychological thinking is itself dependent upon it. Yet the conundrum is based more on logic than on psychologic, on a conception of a definite presence or absence of psychological-mindedness. Rather, the process of analysis exploits and builds upon the capacities for psychological thinking that are available at any given moment. It may be, also, that other capacities such as high motivation and the capacity to form a therapeutic alliance can carry the burden that is successively lightened in favor of increasing facility for psychological-mindedness.

It had been a long and difficult time, this simultaneous use and quest for psychological-mindedness, for Mrs A. and for the analyst. Toward the end of the analysis, she, now 40 years old, dreamed of a woman who just had had a baby advising Mrs A. that in building a house one must be sure to put in windows right from the beginning, as it is so difficult to put them in later. At least for the moment knowing and seeing, Mrs A. asked, "Can we put windows in a 40-year-old house?"

There have been claims that training groups or psychotherapy groups are helpful in encouraging psychological-mindedness, partly through identification with the psychological-mindedness of the peers, the group's cultural sanction, and fewer resistances than might otherwise be mobilized by individual work. The quick regressions characteristic of groups may help to bring forth content, which the group then uses to demonstrate psychological thinking. Something of this sort takes place in every individual analysis, too, no matter how naturally psychologically minded the analysand may be. Psychological-mindedness probably always benefits from training.

The question, "How does one estimate psychological-mindedness?" presumes an answer as to whether one *should* attempt to diagnose such aspects of the personality rather than simply to accept the putative patient, at least for a trial analysis.

Even if one has put aside the old view that all people are the same and that psychoanalysis is the only treatment worthy of the name, there still is the argument that except for people obviously incapable of being analyzed, no one ought to be deprived of the opportunity. One wonders, however, if there is not an element of know-nothingism in this otherwise admirable humanitarian position. Such a point of view really rests on the assumption that a diagnostic examination cannot be made accurate enough to avoid excluding people from analysis who might greatly benefit from it. There are enough disagreements on this point to suggest that this is an empirical question rather than a principle or theory. Such disagreements often reflect great differences in the ability to select patients correctly for analysis and in beliefs in whether to try. In any case, the "trial analysis" seems to be on its way out, according to Diatkine (1968), if for no other reason than saving the patient the feeling of rejection should continued analysis not be feasible. He recommended instead that the analyst draw out the patient as the patient tells his initial story. "In the most satisfactory cases, the patient starts to associate and to realize there are connections between different parts of his discourse . . . on the other hand there are patients who repeat their story without ever enriching it with new meanings" (pp. 267–268). A more pointed method would be to let the patient try thinking psychologically, asking him what he thinks might be the meaning of a certain remark or whether he can see how some of his remarks could pertain to others.

More attention to the process and components of psychological-mindedness should result in more precise examinational techniques. The clinical interview might well be improved by a battery of psychological tests, when a psychologist is available who can make and communicate them helpfully to analysts (Appelbaum 1969, 1970). Many psychological tests are specifically for the elucidation of skills and characteristics relevant to psychological-mindedness. And there are special techniques that offer the patient a standardized opportunity to think psychologically (Luborsky 1953).

Part III

Reflections on Change

Psychotherapy's place in society as an economic commodity can work against the discharge of its practitioners' philosophical and scientific responsibilities. Because of the demand on their time and the substantial rewards for it, psychotherapists, in private practice especially, may focus predominantly on the technical aspects of the discipline, how to practice better, for more people and more efficiently. Such an emphasis may limit contemplative reflection and the sense of paradox, even absurdity, characteristic of so many callings; instead it may lead to the use of words and concepts as if they were immutable objects rather than practical means of solving immediate, pragmatic tasks. The very success of psychotherapy may sometimes indiscriminately seem to confirm all the assertions, assumptions, and practices made in psychotherapy's behalf. Finally, psychotherapy's legal and administrative status tends to isolate it from its inherently existential nature. In the next chapter I shall draw away from psychotherapy as activity in order to understand it better from other angles and to place its participants in positions pertaining more to life than therapy, as contending with values that may strain against the boundaries of a narrowly defined treatment conception of the enterprise. I also shall note that in examining some words and concepts more closely they become more complex and thus for some purposes are less useful but more interesting and, I think, ultimately rewarding.

8

The Paradoxes

Science is perhaps more the pursuit than the discovery of knowledge. It follows the law of successive approximation, chasing an ideal, approaching the truth, but never achieving it. Consequently, the scientific mind is chronically restless. Although complacency feels good and may be refreshing, at times in the scientific quest, it signals the end of scientific questing. By contrast, the signal that scientific work is in progress is the existence of paradoxes, tensions like those disconfirmations that Popper (1959) thought to be the source of scientific growth.

Webster's dictionary defines paradox as, among other things, "a statement that seems contradictory, unbelievable, or absurd, but that may actually be true in fact" and "a statement that is self-contradictory in fact and, hence, false." Thus, a paradox may be true or false (which in itself is paradoxical). Some of the dictionary's synonyms for paradox are "enigma," "mystery," and "ambiguity." Enigmas, mysteries, and ambiguities snap the scientist to attention. The structure of paradox creates a tension that motivates the scientist. The content of the paradox may supply hints to how the tension may be resolved or the directions in which to search for new knowledge. Such "new knowledge" may include discoveries that dispel the false premises or assumptions on which the paradox is based, or it may include new conceptualizations. Either way, as paradox is dissolved, science advances.

John Wisdom (1975) claimed that there is no vital controversy in psychoanalysis at the present and that a science without controversy is moribund. For similar reasons Eissler (1969) took a dim view of the prospects for growth in psychoanalysis. He characterized it as a complacent science in which new data are no longer flowing and whose theory is so loosely organized that it can be bent to explain satisfactorily any and all events. It suffers, he stated, from the absence of paradoxes. Eissler may be right in referring only to those paradoxes that were both created and solved by Freud's great paradigms. He also may be right in implying that many psychoanalysts have comfortably accommodated to what, in the eyes of others, continues to be paradoxical. But aside from these considerations, paradoxes abound in psychoanalysis and psychoanalytic psychotherapy.

Paradox also depends on the fit of its parts to reality. Anyone can claim that he does not believe in or practice one or more of the assertions on which the paradox depends, or he may conceptually explain away the paradox. The following examples of suggested paradox, therefore, may not be paradoxical to some psychotherapists but are offered here as problems, cast in paradoxical terms and based on how the profession is described, taught, and presumably practiced by at least some persons.

PARADOXES IN THE PROFESSION OF PSYCHOTHERAPY

One meaning of "to practice" is to improve one's skill, as when one practices the piano. Much about the practice of psychotherapy conforms to this meaning. It takes a long time to learn how to practice psychotherapy: it should be done with a variety of cases in a variety of situations; the therapist must choose among many kinds and grades of technical interactions; and veteran psychotherapists acknowledge that they continue to learn from every case. Under certain circumstances, with certain patients, and with certain goals in mind, almost anything may "work." Little formal research is available to demonstrate that any one approach is so efficient as to be considered a finished product. One respectable psychoanalytic answer to the demand for research is that every psychoanalysis is a research. In summary, psychotherapy takes place in the absence of formally validated methods or fully consensual thought and is practiced by a kind of perennial student in a research-learning context. The psychotherapist does what he can; the subject does what he can and pays the fee; and both hope for the best. Such an attitude not only conforms to the facts but also encourages the tentativeness and scrutiny characteristic of the psychotherapeutic search for meaning.

Yet "to practice" has a second meaning, as when one practices or applies something already learned. This is what a patient expects in return for his fee. Otherwise he would simply consult with his friends. It is what the patient has expected through the ages from the psychotherapist's predecessors, the witch doctors and the priests. He did not consult them as if they were students learning their trade or trying to find a connection with God but as people who professed to be already equipped with such connections and knowledge. Children turn to their parents not as student-parents or as bumbling hopefuls but as people who, without doubt, can "make it better." This seems to be one means by which "suggestion" works, an often unsung factor in psychotherapy.

The therapist hopes to help the patient understand and overcome, through self-understanding and maturation, faith in his therapist's omnipotence. Yet, paradoxically, many psychotherapists act as if they were indeed practicing a profession that warrants being accepted on faith. Their professional organizations tend to be selective in membership and thought, often functioning as lobbies and guilds to protect and circumscribe the rights and emoluments of their practice and hesitating to consider new points of view. The professionals' social relationships, indeed all their life patterns, may be extensions and extrapolations of the implicit elitist connotations of their titles and their fees. These styles of life are hardly those of earnest students humbly doing what they can, learning from experience, and hoping for the best. They are those of exalted practitioners producing results at high prices. One may ponder what silent price is being exacted from patients and therapists for such clashing images. The answer offered by the human potential movement is that the price is high and that these elitist ways of life must infiltrate and influence relationships with patients. Such attitudes deprive patients of the opportunity to increase their self-esteem and to function autonomously, and they imbue the therapeutic atmosphere with hypocrisy. The strident way in which this position is sometimes expressed ought not to detract from the issue. Psychotherapists, knowing about splitting and isolation, should be able to come to terms with the dangers implicit in trying to encompass two contrasting meanings of the word "practice" in one personality and activity. Among these dangers are unwarranted reductionistic thinking, confusing inferences for facts, and intervening in ways that undercut the patient's capacities. By making practice, profession, and life style more consonant with one another, psychotherapists would probably improve all three.

Here is one attempt at a conceptual solution to this paradox. For better or worse, psychotherapy does conform to both meanings of the word "practice." The psychotherapist does continue to learn, as his knowledge is unfinished, indeed may be in its infancy. Yet, he is no innocent. There is a difference between talking to one's neighbor and talking to a psychotherapist. Many patients are well advised to pay their fee and take their chances with a learner who is, in important respects, a more advanced student than him. Moreover, the professional offers helpful conditions for learning, often unavailable elsewhere.

Without definitive research and consensually validated training and practice, it is understandable that psychotherapy is rife with argument as to which therapeutic approach is better than another. Such arguments may be couched in terms of formal science, philosophy, or values. When psychotherapeutic approaches are defended in general terms, by citing norms, scientific findings, philosophy of science, and generalizations about human nature, one would expect to find members of all schools of psychotherapy espousing each of the various positions. Yet, paradoxically, what one usually finds is that they prefer the school in which they were trained. One may argue that they seek training in what they think is best. Usually, however, as neophytes, they are usually not so well informed. Rather, people often pick a particular field on the basis of unconscious fantasies. Objectivity and generality likely are rationalizations for beliefs that, along with unconscious fantasy, are based emotionally on the feeling of acceptance and identification with the accepters. Each school of behavioral change colludes in this emotional, scientifically premature certainty by choosing which knowledge to teach, shaping it to fit as many situations as possible and often leaving its students uneducated, sometimes in facts themselves, but mainly in epistemology and evaluation of theory and practice.

Coincidentally, everyone has opinions of the other schools, especially of psychoanalysis, even without training or practice in these other disciplines. Yet, paradoxically, most psychotherapists would agree that knowledge is likely to be dependable and useful when it is experiential. Psychotherapy, in particular, is an enterprise that should be experienced in order to be understood. The lesson to be drawn from these paradoxical situations is that comparative judgments among psychotherapies (e.g., Gestalt therapy versus psychoanalysis) and within psychotherapies (e.g., Kleinian versus Freudian) are best stated with the tentativeness appropriate to the lack of direct experiential information and with due regard to the need to believe, which can counter the capacity to assess.

Psychotherapy is variously described as experimental research, an opportunity for understanding the individual, and a cure. The paradox implicit in its being all of these things is usually elided by the position that psychotherapy indeed is all three things at one time. Thus, cure comes while achieving understanding, and in the course of understanding, new knowledge is acquired. This seemingly comfortable position, however, depends upon the belief that the goals and procedures of any one of these enterprises in no way affect the goals and procedures of the others. This assumption has from time to time been challenged. For example, the research attitude is said to distort data and limit inferences because of the researcher's a priori interests. This attitude would tend to introduce a cold, calculating manner that harms the therapeutic relationship, which ought to be marked by warmth and benevolence on the therapist's part.

Changed behavior, which could justifiably be called "cure," can subvert the goal of understanding. (Although Eissler's patient changed her life and was satisfied with her treatment, Eissler considered the treatment a failure because she was not understood psychoanalytically [1963].) In recent years the distinction between understanding and cure has been sharpened and has become a source of criticism of psychoanalytic psychotherapy by behaviorists and human potential therapists. Each of these schools considers understanding irrelevant or inimical to change, improvement, and cure. The therapist may understand his patient, and the patient may understand himself, but this understanding may have little or nothing to do with changed behavior.

The new schools of therapy seek to disturb the complacency of traditional therapists toward these relationships. This complacency is partly shown in the notorious lack of follow-up data. (Yet, in the follow-up section of the Psychotherapy Research Project of the Menninger Foundation, some change two years after the termination of treatment was found to be more the rule than the exception [Horwitz 1974, Appelbaum 1977a].) The relationships among research, understanding, and cure are important questions for psychotherapy. Only by recognizing the paradox of pursuing three different goals by means of one procedure can one be open to the possibility that different goals might determine different procedures.

People speak of the theory and technique of psychotherapy as if they were homogeneous or monolithic, e.g., is psychotherapy helpful, should I have psychotherapy, what is the purpose of psychotherapy? In fact, no two psychotherapies are alike, because no two patients are alike, no two therapists are alike, and therefore no two matches between patient and therapist are alike. What is called psychotherapy may take place in days or in years. It may emphasize sometimes contradictory understandings of personality and use different techniques. When specified by name, such as supportive psychotherapy or expressive psychotherapy, psychoanalytic psychotherapy, or psychoanalysis, one still cannot be sure that those who claim to practice one of these are doing the same thing. Even psychoanalysis, whose basic model is among the most uniform of the treatments, was compared by Freud to a chess game in which the beginning and ending moves could be known, whereas the other moves were subject to great variation. This recognition casts grave doubts on that research in psychotherapy whose design casts psychotherapy as an independent variable. It casts further doubt on such pronouncements as "the patient can (or cannot) benefit from psychotherapy." Paradoxically, psychotherapy is homogeneous only when it is viewed as an administrative unit for legal or insurance purposes or for setting fees; its homogeneity vanishes when it is examined for its substance. One might be able to live comfortably with this paradox if the various understandings of psychotherapy remained homogeneous and functionally pure as used. But the organizational, social, and legal views of psychotherapy sometimes infiltrate the thinking and practice of those who work with its substance. Vicissitudes of the mind-body issue offer examples.

MIND-BODY PARADOXES

In many sectors of psychotherapy, even among many psychoanalysts themselves, the guild position of organized psychoanalysis (it is a medical treatment and therefore cannot be practiced by nonphysicians) has become quaint. It is a dismal fact of life, like the wasteland discharge from a television screen. Freud said it all in *The Question of Lay Analysis* (1926b), and anything he might have missed was supplied by Eissler in his

Medical Orthodoxy and the Future of Psychoanalysis (1965). Freud's medical background was of psychoanalytic use to him solely because it gave him an opportunity to listen to patients, and on the basis of this listening he made his discoveries. Otherwise, it may even have impeded the development of psychoanalysis as we now know it. Freud's medical background encouraged him into taking a detour, the *Project for a Scientific Psychology* (1895a), and was likely responsible for much of the metapsychological and linear reasoning that is now under attack. As recent theoreticians (Holt 1965, Klein 1970, Schafer 1973, 1976) have pointed out, much of this metapsychology can be simply dropped from psychoanalysis without great loss and possibly with great gain. Nothing specific in Freud's medical background seemed to have been responsible for the great and enduring discoveries on which psychoanalysis is built. The same things that are done and thought about under the rubric of medical treatment could also be done under another rubric.

This paradox is further linked to other paradoxes. It is argued that psychoanalysis must remain a medical treatment because the psychoanalyst, as a physician, will know whether something should be treated with psychological or physical means. Yet that same psychoanalyst is prevented from examining the patient himself; he must refer the patient for a physical examination, as any nonphysician would. Indeed, a nonphysician might be more likely to make such a referral than to attempt to use his residual medical skill in diagnosing through superficial observation and interview, as limited by the psychotherapeutic situation. The professional dichotomy based on mind and body has retarded the full appreciation of the unity of mind and body. Although this unity is cited by physicians, it is violated by their practice. Psychologists and psychoanalytically informed psychotherapists conduct, teach, and refine purely psychological interventions, that is, verbal psychotherapy. Ironically, though physicians buttress their claim to hegemony over psychotherapy because of their familiarity with the body, the use of the body in psychotherapy is now being propagated on all sides by mostly nonmedical people—Structural Integration (Rolfing), Neo-Reichian techniques, Feldenkrais and Alexander teachings, and others.

The other major argument for the medical position is that only the physician has been trained to undertake the responsibility for human life. Yet, in some circumstances, the very "taking" of such responsibility for the patient is antitherapeutic in that it undermines the patient's attempts at independence. This latter view is often stated categorically, frequently under the banner of politically democratic values or humanism unleavened by clinical sophistication. Paradoxically, it is both true and untrue that the psychotherapist takes, or should take, responsibility for the patient's welfare. To what extent it is true varies from patient to patient, therapist to therapist, clinical situation to clinical situation, and what is meant by "responsibility." But this can hardly be resolved according to such simplistic, paradoxical declamations.

The most important influences on personality are laid down in the preverbal years, or at least in the years when sensorimotor influences are used relatively more than are verbal skills. Yet we rely upon verbal skills to rediscover and relive these influences. Psychotherapists try to explain away this paradox by maintaining that verbalizing is sufficient to recapture preverbal experiences. "Sufficient," however, is a tricky word unless one is willing to assert that he is entirely satisfied with his results—that they are as good and come as quickly as possible. Short of that assertion, "sufficient" merely stands for a feeling of satisfaction, without knowing what could have been accomplished under other circumstances.

In the preverbal years the child relates himself to the world on the basis of affects, expresses himself through bodily actions, and is guided by physiological reactions. It is an accepted canon of psychotherapeutic technique that what a patient experiences in therapy is most conducive to learning and change when experienced with feeling. Yet how are we to know how much affect is enough? By using standard psychotherapeutic procedures one

one becomes acquainted with a range of affect, and since satisfying results often have been correlated with the upper range,
we assume that in "successful" cases enough affect has been produced. Yet there is increasingly more reason to believe, as
demonstrated by primal scream therapy, feeling therapy,
bioenergetics, and other techniques, that many more and
intense affects are available than usually occur in the psychotherapeutic hours. It might well be that psychotherapeutic
results would be even better if it were possible to introduce
more effective means of recovering affects, particularly those of
the important and determining preverbal years. Since in those
years the body is so central to the child's experience, it is plausible that the body is a repository of such experiences, as is
claimed by proponents of Structural Integration (Rolfing), and
the Alexander and the Feldenkrais techniques. These new interventions would make it possible to avoid the paradox of dealing
verbally with preverbal influences and perhaps to introduce
added power and efficiency to psychotherapy.

Many psychotherapists believe that the effectiveness of
psychoanalytic work, particularly of interpretations, is enhanced
by an altered state of consciousness in the patient. This belief
began with hypnosis. Posthypnotic suggestion, age regression,
and the release of affect all are dependent upon a relatively
primitive level of consciousness. This level of consciousness is
marked by greater receptivity to and absorption with the therapist, to the exclusion of other stimuli and competing points of
view, a relative shift from secondary to primary process, and the
encouragement of spontaneous feeling as opposed to controlled,
filtered, and bound feelings. Psychoanalysts encourage such a
state of mind to some extent by using a couch, and all dynamic
psychotherapists do so, though less, by using a soft voice in a
quiet, unobtrusive room. Yet, paradoxically, psychotherapists
often rely upon their patients' developing information at the
upper, vigilant levels of consciousness. Wandering attention is
often considered resistance; focused attention and concentration
are required if a patient is to grasp the formulations in which

many interpretations are couched. This may be contrasted with those therapies that depend much more on spontaneity, catharsis, and the primitive levels of consciousness induced by drugs and stimulus deprivation. The dynamic psychotherapist may argue that the insights developed by the patient in the more traditional context are more useful because they are integrated by and within the range of consciousness in which ordinary life is usually conducted. Taking this paradox seriously would result, however, in a less complacent exploration of the possibilities. Could it not be that there is an optimal level, combining cognition with a consciousness that is altered toward primitiveness, which would offer psychotherapy greater effectiveness? Not to examine this paradox and not to experiment with the possibilities that stem from it would be to assume that psychotherapy as it now is usually practiced occurs at levels of consciousness that facilitate the process. That may be the correct answer, but first the question has to be asked.

DETERMINISM–CHOICE PARADOXES

Psychoanalysis teaches us that all behavior is determined. Yet, paradoxically, the behaviors that comprise psychoanalysis are designed to overcome much that determines, in order to allow increased choice. How does one choose to escape unconscious determinism if one's choice to do so is unconsciously determined? Like the man on the Cream of Wheat box holding up a box on which there is the picture of the man on the Cream of Wheat box, *ad infinitum*, overcoming determined behavior is itself determined and overcoming that determination is itself determined *ad infinitum*. One way this problem has been handled is through hypothesizing agencies of the mind that are free of unconscious determination, e.g., Hartmann's secondary autonomy. But this metapsychological sleight-of-hand implies that there is a sharper line between unconsciously determined and consciously determined behavior than there really is and further may imply to some people that it is possible to remove unconsciously determined behavior. This belief can lead to interminable analyses, during which a complete knowledge of unconscious motivation is pursued in the hope that it will result in change. Schafer (1973, 1976) and Wheelis (1950, 1956, 1973), among others, argued for a psychoanalytic psychology of choice and will. They implied that a person is relatively free of unconscious determination and that this freedom is exploited by the person's application of will power and conscious intent, often despite the continuing tug of "neurotic" trends. In their view the only way to produce change is by behaving differently, that people behave in response to different influences of varying levels of awareness and that awareness must be harnessed to execution. Together with unconscious determinism, old-fashioned determination deserves an honored role in psychotherapy.

Reason detached from choice and consequent action would be merely scholasticism. Freud (who did many things with patients that contradict his writings on technique) surely had in mind practical reasonableness when he established the primacy of reason in his theory. Determination and changed behavior can still be unconsciously determined to some extent, as can those behaviors that are changed through treatment. A psychology of choice and action, which Hartmann (1964b) felt we lack, would be the only escape from a theory that suggests that a person can function without unconscious determination, even as he is said to behave as a function of unconscious determinism.

That all behavior is determined is a comforting thought. If one can ascertain motives, he may be able to control his destiny — all things may be possible, albeit determined. But, paradoxically, life is also a game of chance, a series of adventures and misadventures based on accidents and the unforeseen. We can look backwards and downwards for motives, but we can never look ahead and be sure of the consequences of our actions. Some criticisms of psychotherapy founder on this sometimes overlooked fact. Some people seem to assume that there is a direct line from the psychotherapeutic experience to "results," as these can be observed in the way a person subsequently lives.

But the way a person lives is only partly dependent upon the extent to which he is able to control his destiny; it is also partly dependent upon the destinies of others, nature, and statistics. Life and behavior are determined and they follow laws, but in a context of randomness and chance.

PARADOXES IN VALUES

Perhaps the paradox best able to generate continued thought and to influence action and thus change in psychotherapy pertains to values. Let us imagine a patient in psychotherapy who is capable of being as expressive as we can help him to be without his becoming suicidal or psychotic. For such a patient the main objective of psychotherapy is to help him make up his own mind and to expand his choices, in part by clarifying how he selects choices, or selects values. For such a patient, what psychotherapy offers is not merely to remove his symptoms, turn him into a good citizen, or make him a productive person, but the freedom to choose how he wants to live. In many respects psychotherapy is ideal for such a patient. Psychotherapy was originally designed by Freud as an objective, valueless, neutral therapy to help counteract the moral condemnations of patients with neurotic symptoms and to encourage patients to feel free to say what was on their mind without fear of being harshly judged. Freud supported this objectivity and neutrality, as found in his statement (1933) that psychoanalysis as a branch of science had only a scientific *weltanschauung*, or way of viewing life. There was no need for psychoanalysis to take a moral position or subscribe to any value other than the search for truth. Indeed, values offered by the psychoanalytic therapist, explicitly or implicitly, interfere with the means of treatment and run counter to the ends of the treatment.

Paradoxically, however, psychotherapists do offer a priori values that by definition limit free choice and may impede self-awareness. These values stem from the process itself, in part from its sociocultural context and in part from some psychotherapists' satisfaction that because they do not moralize they are not suggesting values to their patients.

What might be called functional values are inherent in psychotherapy. They include the rules and regulations, with their concomitant attitudes and consequent behaviors, that make the task possible. For example, psychotherapy relies on the patient's giving up or reducing his resistances, on being honest, and on talking freely. The patient may, of course, do none of these things, and he has the right not to do so. So long as he pays the fee he may continue to come to the hours for any reason—to avoid acting and making decisions, to tell others that he is in psychotherapy, or to listen to himself talk. The therapist may not object to earning his money and using his time in these ways, but he does have the responsibility to show the patient that he is not using his hours in the way that the psychotherapist believes would most benefit him, produce the most changes, and move the process along most expeditiously. The patient cannot have it both ways. If he wants expressive psychotherapy, he has to work so as to allow it to take place. The patient learns, therefore, that the psychotherapist values openness, honesty, and psychological thinking, that isolating affect from thought, blotting out the present, being unable to remember the past are not helpful, and that certain kinds of information and attitudes are more useful than others. The patient learns the esteem in which self-knowledge is held and the belief that truth will set people free, that good interpersonal relationships are helpful experiences, and behavior follows laws which can be learned.

Human potential psychotherapists suggest that the patient pays a high price for yielding to such conditions. According to them, patients have an inner wisdom that frees them of resistances when they are ready. They believe that examining such resistances is a form of controlling the patient and leads only to intellectualization. Overstated and often erroneous, these criticisms do call attention to the paradox of a value-laden psychotherapy founded on neutrality. If this paradox is not examined, the result may be an atmosphere of arbitrariness and imposition that opposes expressive psychotherapy and the patient's quest for autonomy and choice.

The greatest contributions of psychoanalytic psychotherapy are its focus on man's idiosyncratic nature and its teaching that no behavior can be assessed without knowing its meaning to the patient. Yet, despite these individual differences, social, and therefore by definition, general values are often held as the criteria for success. For example, case reports often conclude triumphantly with the information that the patient married, had children, went back to school, or became more productive at work. It is as if these conventional social goals are equivalent to the criteria for successful treatment. If the patient shares such impressions, he will be deprived of being able to decide for himself how his live should be lived. Moreover, striving for or acting upon such values may lead him into situations in which, enlightened though he may be, he is worse off than before. Symptoms, neuroses, and deviant life styles, after all, are not necessarily the worst of all possible eventualities; by definition they are compromises and therefore may be better than what would happen without such compromises, for example, depression, suicide, antisocial action, or making others miserable. If the psychotherapist holds social values as criteria for success, he will have difficulty giving equal time and equal effort to all aspects of all issues that might yield awareness.

It is easy for some therapists to accept as adequately analyzed those decisions that fit his social values. For example, the patient may announce that he is going to rob a bank, get a divorce, or commit suicide. The therapist says, O.K., it's a free country, but perhaps we ought to see what your motives are before you take such action. In so doing, the patient and the therapist may learn much about the motives that have prompted this idea. Then, one day, the patient announces that he is not going to rob a bank, get divorced, or commit suicide, after all. The therapist may understandably be relieved; he may be less inclined to pursue the motives for this socially sanctioned decision with the assiduousness he brought to bear on the socially deviant one. In the social context in which the therapist works, he will be blamed if his patients rob banks, get divorced, or commit suicide. In principle, however, there may be conscious or unconscious motives unknown to the therapist for these new, socially condoned decisions. The patient may be attempting to please the therapist or to set up the therapist for later and greater disappointments; his accomplices may have backed down; or as a prisoner of social conformity he may just have lost his nerve, not only to rob banks, get divorced, or commit suicide, but also to think different and creative thoughts. To psychotherapy such questions as, Why not rob a bank? and Why remain married? may be revealing and deserve equal time. If, for example, a person cannot answer the question, Why not commit suicide? he is probably handicapped in living the life he holds on to.

I am asserting here a morality of freedom as a context in which therapy should always take place. This morality is not to be confused with inner freedom, the capacity to make decisions free, or relatively free, of unconscious influences. Those people who decide to rob a bank, drop a bomb, or commit suicide probably do not have much inner freedom or much awareness of their motives. Yet their intentions must be considered as honorable within the context of the morality of freedom. These intentions should therefore be treated honestly, objectively, and without prejudices (other than the assumption that they lack awareness in order to come to conclusions that have such heavy prices attached to them).

Health values include the notions that patients should become normal, whole, self-actualizing, genital characters or have generative personalities. These are romantic ideals, abstractions that one may strive for but never achieve. Let us be satisfied, Freud (1895b) said, with transforming "hysterical misery into common unhappiness" (p. 305). If patients and therapists believe that the romantic ideals of mental health are real, they may impose a secondary guilt upon the infantile sources of guilt. The patient feels, in effect, "I should not be neurotic; I should not behave badly; I have had the advantages of psychotherapy." The therapist himself may also feel like a failure, gradually, reluctantly, and perhaps cynically lowering sights that need not have been so high in the first place. This is not to say that there are no technical standards by which to judge psychological development, the functioning of the ego, object relations, and change in all of these. The problems are in assuming that all people can achieve the highest standards and that if they cannot, the psychotherapy has not been a success.

Values are inherent in the stance that the psychotherapist takes with his patient. Rather than being stick or mirror, the therapist devotes his time and energy to such assumptions as life is better than death (and therefore suicide should not be an option), he is concerned for the other person's best interests, and happiness is better than unhappiness. Necessary as these beliefs may be for a helpful human relationship and for conditions in which change can come about, they are subject to the paradox that the patient's choice is likely to end when his therapist reveals that these are also his values. If, for example, the therapist and patient agree beforehand that the therapist has the best interests of the patient at heart, it becomes difficult to expose, and therefore understand, the patient's distress, cynicism, or despair that such a thing is possible. If they accept without question that happiness is better than unhappiness, it becomes difficult to understand that happiness cannot infringe upon the happiness of others and that without adjusting to this fact the patient is on the road to narcissism. Without examining these issues it becomes difficult to understand that certain kinds of happiness are passports to nowhere and that certain kinds of unhappiness can be honored as a breeding ground for creativity and change.

Cultural values may impinge on the process. The therapist may tell the patient that he will intercede if the patient is going to commit murder or throw a bomb. He may stand for, but not analyze, a variety of other cultural taboos. Paradoxically, however, culture, according to Freud (1930), was set up in opposition to the individual; to exercise full freedom of choice, the individual should be able to examine all aspects of culture, which by definition have diminished his freedom. Whether or not to practice incest, cannibalism, or murder are, from this point of view, legitimate questions for dispassionate analysis. At the heart of psychoanalysis is the belief that all is relative, nothing is in principle given, and one must know meanings and circumstances before coming to conclusions. Only then can one resolve the paradox of a process whose goal is free choice being hedged in by choices already made.

PARADOXES IN THE NATURE AND GOALS OF PSYCHOTHERAPY

A person who wants help with his life now has many choices. He can consider various counterculture, human potential interventions which are relatively inexpensive in that they take place during brief periods of time and usually on an as-needed basis. Or he may consider choosing long-term psychotherapy which is expensive in both time and money, with the general expectation that years will elapse before an ending can be expected. Although the patient may have many unconscious reasons for choosing one or another, if he chooses long-term psychotherapy, his conscious expectation is that the greater investment of time and money will have better results. Presumably, he is seeking some form of happiness, whether relief from symptoms or changes in the way he feels or lives. If he views this intervention as treatment, consciously or unconsciously, he will find a fixed beginning and ending familiar. He has been encouraged through the years to believe that if one goes to a doctor for treatment, when the treatment is over the difficulties that brought him will also be over. Unless he has an incurable disease, he will expect the treatment to be definitive. This impression is helped along if the psychotherapist is called doctor and if the psychotherapy takes place in a medical institution or in an office modeled after those of other private medical practitioners he has seen. Much is right about his expectations. If it were not so, it would indeed be better for him to invest far less time and money in some other intervention.

Yet, paradoxically, the theory of the psychotherapist contradicts what is implied by his offering himself as a "treater" of "illness." Instincts, unlike infections, are ineradicable; conflicts, unlike fractures, are ordinarily less "healed" in the absolute sense of being resolved than adapted to or managed through changes in impulse-defense configurations. Psychological change, unlike recovery from an appendectomy, raises new questions and poses new challenges, which may produce even more unhappiness than did the less demanding challenges of the symptoms that brought the patient to therapy in the first place. Indeed, new and increased misery is expected during the course of expressive psychotherapy. Psychoanalysts act on the understanding of the substantive interminability of analysis when they require analysis for training purposes, even though, and often not long after, a candidate has "finished" three to five years of a personal analysis. Indeed, it would come as no surprise if some number of analysands could, after completing their analyses, apply to a diagnostic clinic, detail their dissatisfactions with life, tell of their symptoms, describe their feelings and their concern about life and where they are going, and have analysis recommended for them. It is probable that the analysis would be predicted to require, and would in fact last, three to five years. Paradoxically, these patients might have benefited greatly from their previous analyses.

The general assumption that long-term psychotherapy is a definitive "treatment" is further confirmed by the lack of provision for continued or repeated therapy. The patient can, of course, return after "ending" his treatment. And yet he may be reluctant to do so, perhaps even feel guilty of malingering or excessive dependence should he require further therapy. He has, after all, just spent thousands of dollars and many years for the most expensive, intensive, and definitive treatment available. And he was supposed to have learned how to do self-analysis in the process.

Neurosis is, to some degree, a function of how one looks at one's life. Therapy usually begins with morbidity as the figure, with what is good about one's situation as the ground. "Cure" may result from, or be signaled by, a reversal of this relationship. The patient role is exchanged for the ex-patient role. What was presented in terms of "I can't" becomes "I won't" or "I will."

Instead of stating that some things in life offer satisfaction but life in general is miserable, the patient says that some things are still miserable but life in general is rewarding. This is not different from what usually occurs for most people: good days and bad days, days when nothing seems right, and days when everything seems fine, though nothing has changed externally that would distinguish the two.

All behavior has meaning and performs a function. Thus, one can look at behavior for its advantages, its use as an adaptation, its healthfulness or its goodness — or one can look at it for its disadvantages. In the latter view, behavior would be labeled sick or at least maladaptive. Although a successful course of treatment is likely to change the balance — the contributions of helpful attitudes and behaviors as opposed to harmful ones — that one's life is a point of view does not change. Indeed, an unchanging point of view, whether optimistic or pessimistic, may be a sign of rigid defensiveness.

Paradoxically, many human potential supporters who do not concern themselves with repression or instincts and believe in man's goodness and perfectability act as if they do recognize the insolubility of intrapsychic difficulties. They accept as a matter of course that people have to be experientially reminded of their internal workings and to be kept open to the possibility of new solutions. Their intermittent interventions are recognitions that "psychotherapy" is a lifelong struggle. By contrast, long-term psychotherapists, who with Freud tend to view man as needing to overcome his fundamentally evil drives and to accept a tragic view of reality (Schafer 1970), nonetheless stipulate sharp boundaries between treatment and life, speak of the beginnings and endings of treatment, and implicitly promise that the treatment will justify the investment it requires.

A major task of the termination of psychotherapy is to resolve the transference, whether this be the transference neurosis of analysis or the less integrated and intense and more sporadic transference effects of psychotherapy. Those aspects of the relationship modeled and emotionally colored by relationships with past figures should be sufficiently worked through so that the ex-patient can relate to his ex-therapist as he does to other people. He can carry with him memories of the analyst untainted by emotions felt toward him that derived from his past. He is free to do self-analysis for realistic purposes, neither slavishly nor out of exaggerated needfulness, anger, rebellion, or hopelessness.

And yet, paradoxically, would the therapist and patient enter into a business transaction or social relationship the day after the therapy terminated? They probably would be well advised not to, for the relationship has not been resolved in an absolute sense. What would be an appropriate interval before they could have an ordinary social relationship — weeks, months, years? Some seasoned psychotherapists say that they prefer not to socialize or enter into sensitive business relationships with ex-patients until several years have passed. Ordinary observation, if not introspection, leads to the conclusion that the patient's unrealistic ideas and feelings modeled on and intensified by the past that he has attached to his therapist may persist for many years, perhaps indefinitely.

An examination of this paradox would lead to a study of what is meant by the term "resolution" and would probably result in an overhaul of that and other absolutist terms in psychotherapy. Indeed, much of the language of psychotherapy is overstated in its implications of definitiveness and closure. Words denoting tentativeness and relativity, which conform to the openness of the system, would better fit the facts. One finding from the test examinations in the Psychotherapy Research Project of the Menninger Foundation was that conflicts changed after psychotherapy in a variety of ways, but few of them could be considered resolved (Appelbaum 1977a).

An examination of this paradox might also help to formulate a better answer to the current criticism that psychotherapists manipulate, control, and influence their patients. An incomplete resolution of the transference, with the consequent maintenance of the patient-therapist relationship beyond the treatment, does provide a plausible avenue for continued influence. Simply hiding behind the language in an effort to deny this observation can only encourage the proliferation and exaggeration of such criticisms. Psychotherapists can be complacent about this paradox only as long as they continue to maintain that they in no way communicate their values to patients, that their values have a beneficial influence on patients anyway, or that these influences end when the treatment ends. These positions should be critically studied.

Many psychotherapists acknowledge that they do not offer a definitive intervention, neither in time nor completeness. The belief that they do, they say, is one that their patients hold, modeled on previous experiences with physicians and rooted in childhood fantasies of happy endings and the fulfillment of wishes. They might mention that Freud recommended reanalysis every five years. But, in view of such modest claims, how do psychotherapists justify the great amount of time and money that psychotherapy requires, as compared to other therapies? The answers lie in a new psychology of happiness and in an understanding of challenges, commitments, and values which would take into consideration levels of development and living, each with its satisfactions and risks. But such a psychology cannot be forthcoming as long as psychotherapists live comfortably with and explain away the paradox that while they appear to offer a definitive course of treatment with definite goals, they also recognize that this is impossible.

From the standpoint of the therapist as observer, psychotherapy is a self-exploration that results in new self-knowledge. This may or may not be true according to the ex-patient's experience. A patient may say that he has learned a great deal about himself, which may be a way of saying that he has been a good patient, that he has learned his ideological catechism, that he likes the therapist, or that he is unconsciously relieved at having gotten away with incomplete knowledge of himself. But even if none of this defensive activity is relevant and his statement genuinely reflects the great amount of self-knowledge that he has achieved, paradoxically this statement will still be as false as it is true. Because of, and as part of, his learning about himself, the patient has at the same time been freed to ask more questions.

He is open to issues and perspectives that he may never have dreamed existed. He owns up to competing points of view because he has examined conflicts. He considers, and therefore questions, options that were previously unthinkable for him. Through deciding about them he is forced into examining his priorities and their related moralities. He must anticipate more consequences and does so through introspective extrapolation from what he already knows of himself. Since he has learned to mistrust the easy or obvious answer, to question motivations, and to want to know, he is able to live with ambiguity. He has embarked on a quest that has no ending. Self-knowledge, like normality and health, are not prizes to be won. Rather, he has learned the rules and has begun to play a game that has no ending, whose players are forever changing. The more learned, the less known is his postanalytic fate, just as the termination of analysis is less an ending than a new beginning. The more one is aware of this paradox and works through it, the more one is likely to be successful in self-analysis. One will then recognize new situations, for which the existing knowledge of self may be insufficient, and one will be open and eager to continue to learn.

I have hardly exhausted the list of paradoxes in psychotherapy's mysterious calling. I hope I have illustrated sufficiently that the restless, willing scientist can find much to conceptualize and experiment with in its theory and practice. Without inquiry, psychotherapy is in danger of slipping into a congealed orthodoxy that may, paradoxically, inflict a fatal disease of old age on a mere youth.

9

The Effect on Change of Idealizing Mental Health

In any enterprise, including psychotherapy, what one does is determined by what one is trying to achieve. When selecting among innumerable possibilities, people are guided by fantasies of what things should or could be. These fantasies have a wish-fulfilling, dreamlike character; for example, the notion that any American baby can grow up to be president, the implicit assumption promulgated by mass communications, that whatever is advertised can belong to anyone, or the myth of the perfect family—white, wealthy, healthy, loving, and lucky. As measured against such ideal notions, many people feel chronically deprived and dissatisfied because of their wishful expectations that they should be what they are not and never can be. A job is unfulfilling because the employee is not president of the company, the wife is disappointing because she fails to look like a movie star, and the children are neither beauty queens nor quarterbacks.

In psychotherapy the guiding fantasy is some explicit or implicit conception of mental health. Such conceptions influence and help to organize the work that is done in therapy and when the treatment ends. A patient's notion of mental health may be that he will have no symptoms, which is serviceable enough if he began treatment with crystallized symptoms. Most patients, however, complain less of specific symptoms than of the quality of life, particularly the nature of interpersonal relationships. Mental health is difficult to measure in these terms and often becomes defined according to the psychotherapist's view of healthy living, which may conflict with those of the patient, be somewhat capricious, or be mindlessly dictated by social modes. Another conception is that mental health is normative: people should behave like normal people, that is, like everyone else. One need only take a close look at the way everyone else behaves to discern the problem with this point of view.

Many psychotherapists opt for what are, in effect, developmental criteria for mental health. The psychoanalytic-developmental point of view is based securely on Freud's psychosexual stages. The child progresses upward in a grand condensation of biopsychological stimuli centering on successive bodily parts, physiological development, interpersonal experience, and social learning. "Upward" is understood in this context as referring to the solution of conflicting tendencies, which arise at successive levels of development. Thus, in more or less chronological order, the healthy child solves issues of survival; the often stubborn and angry emergence of self preparatory to establishing a sense of control and autonomy; and sexual, familial, and social identities, finally arriving at what Freud named as the goal of life, to be able to love and to work. Facets of this scheme are discussed by Werner (1948), Piaget (1954), and Mahler et al. (1975), among others. Erikson (1953) extended and elaborated Freud's psychosexual scheme to include the delineations of character, as influenced by and expressed through social modes. His ideal end point is the "generative stage," the overcoming of narcissism or self-absorption in favor of caring, giving, productive relationships with other people as individuals and as organized in family and social groups. The generative person who has achieved what Erikson calls "integrity" has sufficiently accepted himself and the nature of the world around him to create and contribute to the world out of a sense of "belief in the species," with his contribution being a "welcome trust of the community."

Note that these developmental schemes are stated in general and theoretical as well as in practical terms. Although they offer empirical descriptions of behavior at points along each developmental line, no assumption is offered that any particular developmental point, particularly the highest one, can be attained by everyone. Indeed, descriptions of behavior patterns different from those associated with the ideal, theoretical end point are all too familiar. We easily recognize oral, anal, and phallic characters or masochistic and narcissistic personalities.

In using a developmentally based definition of mental health as a guide to making and ending therapeutic efforts, two essential errors may be made: aiming too low, perhaps out of a sense of despair or disillusionment; or aiming too high, in thrall to wish-fulfilling idealization. The latter, a tendency to act as if the patient will achieve goals that are beyond his or her reach or which may exist in theory or in wish-fulfilling fantasy, occurs more often. What are the reasons for such wish-fulfilling fantasies? The psychotherapist may apply a medical standard, modeled on bodily readings that offer clear measures of health, deviations from which automatically result in prescriptions for treatment. The psychotherapist may be heavily influenced by cultural norms of American idealism and pragmatism, in which it is natural to assume that if something is wrong it can be fixed or that there is always a new frontier over the horizon which can be reached with the exercise of ingenuity and enterprise. To the extent that the psychotherapist's self-esteem is determined by the patient's behavior, he may not accept a patient's decision to remain homosexual, get divorced, drop out of school, or settle for low-paying work. Finally, the psychotherapist, like all people, has lived through and been influenced by an early period in life when everything seemed possible and when "magic" was commonplace, when one was the center of a universe that often satisfied needs and which therefore held the promise of doing so forever. A residual of that phase is the nascent expectation of perfection.

How is idealization accomplished and what tricks of the mind must be played in order to act upon unrealistic fantasies of perfection? One trick is to obscure individual differences; to take general descriptions of personality as being necessarily descriptive of any mentally healthy person. For example, words and concepts like individuation, maturation, adulthood, independence, masculinity or femininity, resolution of conflict, and object libido may be assumed to be good for everybody under all circumstances, and achievable by everybody under all circumstances. Implicit in such thinking is a refusal to face the implications of the determinism, of varying genetic and environmental influences.

Consider, for example, the sibling constellation work of Walter Toman (1976), a point of view supported by dozens of research studies in several countries. Toman assumes conventionally that the first years of life have determining effects on the rest of one's life. Thus, the various sibling constellations that people grow up with result in highly individual choices and experiences in later life. For example, using only data on age and sex of siblings of marital partners, and based on the partners' respective sibling positions, Toman can predict the likelihood of divorce or whether marital difficulties will be those of sex or dominance. The marriage least likely to end in divorce is that of an older brother of a younger sister married to a younger sister of an older brother, and there is an even better chance of harmony if each has parents in positions identical to theirs. Obviously, most people are not in such a favored marital position.

When people first learn of Toman's predictions, they usually respond with depression or anger, or with a joking denial of such feelings. They may be troubled by the determinism of a scheme that confronts them with inherent limitations. Everyone is aware of individual differences in abilities, preferences, and character traits. Although they know better, however, people seem to nourish the fantasy that they are in control of their fate and do not face the world with predetermined limitations or handicaps. To expect a single, ideal end point from people in all sibling positions is to deny the facts, which is exactly what many people do.

Another means of pursuing an unwarranted idealization of mental health is to believe at least covertly that patients will, in fact, achieve ideal goals if given sufficient time and therapeutic skill. While psychoanalytic psychotherapy has few unblemished studies of effectiveness at and after termination, there is persuasive research evidence that psychoanalytic therapy often falls short of the developmental ideal. For example, the Psychotherapy Research Project of the Menninger Foundation, the study of over ten years of psychotherapy, including psychoanalysis, showed that results were less than glowing. How much people improved depended on what intrapsychic assets they had to begin with: the better-endowed patients improved more than the less-endowed ones. Conflicts were not resolved, although they were often reduced in intensity (Appelbaum 1977a).

Anecdotal evidence and common observation are at least as persuasive in this instance as research findings. How many of us would be willing to say that as a group, analyzed people are free of struggle, conflict, and imperfection — that they characteristically behave according to Erikson's descriptions of generativity and integrity?

One consequence of idealizing mental health as the goal of psychotherapy is to prolong treatment unnecessarily. Often such a prolongation is influenced by an idealization of insight: one or both parties continue to pursue insight, believing that just around the corner lies the decisive understanding that will make everything right (Appelbaum, 1975a, 1979a).

Another consequence of misguided perfectionism is that the treatment becomes influenced by the primitive aspects of the superego. What does it mean to the patient to continue to slog away year after year to find imperfections and weaknesses in himself and to notice the distance between what he feels he is supposed to achieve and what he does in fact achieve? Iatrogenic guilt is added to infantile guilt. It is difficult to analyze such situational guilt when the analytic process itself is its reinforcing source. Moreover, such guilt perpetuates itself; it actively inhibits the gratifications of a realistic acceptance of self and behavior. Instead of savoring whatever is achieved, the patient feels admonished to do more and to be better. The patient not only fails to achieve an ideal, but also regards this failure as proof of his imperfections; life as he currently lives it is implicitly downgraded and in that context sours even beyond any difficulties otherwise inherent in it. Although an idealization of mental health purports to encourage therapeutic work, paradoxically such an idealization may discourage it. Beating one's head against a stone wall disposes one to give up in despair, however subtly that despair may be acted upon or expressed.

Another consequence of fantasizing an idealized self may be to encourage posttreatment passivity: once perfection has been achieved in fantasy, it is no longer necessary to work on one's self and relationships. By contrast, the setting of realistic goals, based on the acceptance of imperfection, carries with it the challenge of adaptation, the need to make do despite one's limitations. In response to this challenge, the patient can enjoy running a five-minute mile, free of the wasted effort of trying to run a four-minute mile and free of self-flagellation for not doing so. This is one way of understanding the otherwise surprising happiness of many seriously handicapped people. Rather than fruitlessly striving, the patient's work is to accept himself, to plan accordingly, and to work through fantasies of idealization and omnipotence.

Still another consequence of pursuing idealized fantasies of mental health is to encourage people to get into situations for which they may be ill equipped. Patients may get married, have children, go to school, and change occupations while fantasizing that they are "healthy," only to fail because they have attempted tasks for which they are unsuited, perhaps because of a wish to please the therapist and to live up to an ideal of mental health. In such situations social desires have become intrapsychic desires. Nomothetic standards founded on social values have superseded neutrality. Such lack of neutrality has interfered with the intrapsychic assessment on which goals for any one person should be based. In principle, any goal, not just the "highest" one, can serve as a dangerous idealization for some people, permeated with unreality, stimulating guilt, and encouraging unwarranted effort. Depending upon the major psychosexual challenge, the idealized end point can be confidence in basic survival; feelings of separateness, rightness, and goodness; preening oneself exhibitionistically; or confidence in sexual identity and prowess. Idealization may influence one's choice of mate, occupation, or hobby — any activity adapted more from unrealistic fantasy than from an objective evaluation of the facts or from realizable fantasy. The further an ideal is from one's capability, the greater will be the guilt, disappointment, and frustrated effort. A process conducted according to such infantile modes of experience as unwarranted idealization and irrational guilt, yet having a goal of ridding the patient of infantile modes of experience, produces a bizarrely self-defeating paradox.

That the concept of mental health can be harmfully idealized does not mean that we should do away with such a concept. It does mean that mental health should be conceived of in a way that is helpful rather than dangerous to self-investigation and should contribute to a reasonable and realizable plan of life and treatment. One such way might take its cue from the aphorism that mental health is something that everybody strives for and nobody achieves. In such a formulation mental health becomes a touchstone, a theoretical end point on a scale rather than a moral or technical imperative. Lawrence Kubie (1958) used such a formulation for mental health in his conception of normality. He argued that mental health, or normality, could exist only if all of the unconscious were known; a person could be normal only if he were able to behave totally free of unconscious influences. That ideal state remains something to be striven for, but never with the expectation of achieving it. When a person places himself somewhere on a scale with an ideal of mental health as a theoretical end point rather than as an unquestioned demand, he has a perspective according to which he can determine how to expend his efforts.

But what about resistance? Patients regularly misjudge their capacities, so as to avoid the anxiety of facing their fears of failure or success. How does one know whether a goal of psychotherapy fits the circumstances of the patient or is set too low in the service of resistance? The answer is to be able to judge correctly so as to avoid either pursuing an idealization fruitlessly and harmfully or failing to take on reasonable challenges out of unexamined self-indulgence or to fend off the anxiety of continued development. Here I have emphasized the error of harmfully pursuing idealization because I believe that that is the one less likely to be considered. The training of therapists alert them to the dangers of resistance, to recognize behavior that is slowing, stalling, or reversing the upward developmental process. Less often, psychotherapists and patients recognize the degree to which they pursue nomothetic idealizations.

The challenge of determining what the patient is capable of, when he is harmfully limiting himself, and what is well-founded resistance that ought to be respected as the patient's correct and efficient way of protecting himself and using himself adaptively is often difficult. It poses a problem akin to that of differentiating between acting out and action. Such assessments may be influenced in mischievous ways. Because of infantile expectations and sociomedical pressures for "cure," one can easily forget that all things are not possible for all persons. This is so even though psychotherapists act upon the knowledge of individual differences when they select patients to be in a psychotherapy of greater or lesser expressiveness; when, however informally, they consider some patients to be "good patients" — for whom they have high hopes for achieving a way of life that at least approaches the ideal — or "bad patients" — for whom they have severely limited hopes. If such judgments are possible from the beginning, then they will be possible all the way through the treatment.

When the therapist and the patient each make an assessment, rather than accepting abstract idealized standards, they force themselves to consider the compatibility of goals and capabilities. Is the patient equipped with those functions that make a given goal reasonable? If not, could he so equip himself if repressions were lifted and inhibitions overcome? To what extent does the patient really want to achieve the goals often held by others or society to be desirable? Such an approach requires an existential analysis of oneself and of the social environment. It demands that one make the whole of life a percept and see it in its entirety from a distance that allows perspective and evaluation; that one confront one's death and one's place in the universe and decide how one wants to spend his remaining years. By synthesizing the many, often conflicting, answers to such questions the patient works to achieve integrity. Such integrity may not be to everyone's, or indeed to anyone's, liking. It may be short of ideal standards, or it may be heavily influenced by infantile modes. But the point is that it considers all aspects of the person—his capacities and needs and his values and wishes—in the attempt to align them with each other and with the social environment. The criterion for success is a created synthesis rather than a meeting of a priori demands.

The implementation of such an approach requires increased attention to the problems of adaptation. Some people assume that adaptation is more or less identical with taking it easy, that it is synonymous with giving up or complacency. That is far from true. True adaptation may require work as hard as that designed to achieve developmentally higher goals. That work may be analytic, such as working through fantasies of omnipotence or of the need to please others. Or it may require strengthening defenses or using identification with the therapist or other supportive means by which people change.

The following is a clinical example of the point of view offered in this chapter.

A never married woman in her early thirties with a history of tempestous, unsatisfactory relationships with men was planning to be married. Other significant men in the patient's life—father, brother, and boy friends—had been powerful if not sadistic and played upon the patient's feelings of inferiority. By contrast, the man with whom she was now contemplating marriage was gentle and considerate of her, and he offered her immediate and unstinting love and admiration. He was, however, inferior to her occupationally and financially. In about the 150th hour of treatment the patient had the following two dreams: (1) She was in love with a man with whom she worked, largely because of his great intellect. (2) Two women patients met and fell in love in a hospital and decided to get married. With the help of her associations the two dreams could be taken to reflect the kinds of love objects that she was considering. The first told of her subsidiary, admiring position with regard to men of power. She enjoyed such men but was made anxious by them and felt inferior to them. The second dream implied that she and her fiancé were viewed as being ill, or needful. They had found fulfillment in each other, and she was at ease with this man whom she regarded as less than a man, felt better about herself as a person because of their love for each other, but she had to give up the fantasy of partaking of the power and capability of a man whom she saw as her superior.

The patient was troubled by the implications of the dream; the date of her projected wedding was approaching, and she felt she needed to make a final decision about it (the issues in making such decisions in the course of psychotherapy had been discussed with the patient but are disregarded in this clinical illustration). Two paths beckoned to her: one path was to recognize that her difficulties with self-esteem were neurotic and led to unnecessary anxiety, that her attraction to powerful men was founded on early sadomasochistic experiences. Through self-knowledge she should be able to overcome these difficulties and so find a powerful, admirable man whose talents and capabilities she can comfortably enjoy. The other path was to assume that she could probably never sufficiently overcome her difficulties with self-esteem and her anxiety with powerful, seemingly superior men; she should choose the less-powerful man and enjoy being comfortable with him. Should she fail to make the definitive intrapsychic changes necessary to relate to a man who is ideal to her, she may lose her fiancé, and she may enter into a marriage with someone else that will be marked by the same kinds of tempestous, painful experiences that have typified previous relationships with admired men. But should she choose the "lesser man" she will have to contend with missing the excitement of superior power in her partner.

Ideally, she should take the first path. She should assume that she will overcome her limitations and be able to relate happily to the man of her lifelong dreams. If her current boy friend refused to wait, she should let him go, confident that her difficulties will eventually be worked through successfully and that he will be replaced by a more fully satisfying person. Is the latter course of action merely idealization, impractical, never to be achieved to the degree that would make such an object-choice enduringly gratifying? Should recognizing the existence of neurotic inhibitions automatically gear the psychotherapy and her life to decisions slanted toward the goal and expectation of fully overcoming such inhibitions? Or should the patient resign herself to such inhibitions, choose to marry her current boy friend, enjoy what he has to offer, and come to terms with what may always be missing from her life? In working out such decisions, one should consider the patient's difficult early years; the diagnostic understanding of her as ascertained from psychological tests and interviews and as confirmed during the treatment; her capacities for pain and joy; the likely demands from her current and possibly future socioeconomic environment; and the expectations of significant figures in her life as those are lodged in her self-expectations and self-estimates.

She may or may not choose what ultimately will be the better of the two paths, but her chances of doing so are greatly improved by the work of making that decision, by recognizing what is likely to be gained and lost, and by increased knowledge of the various and conflicting aspects of her personality that affect her decision. Such self-exploration would have been avoided had she simply assumed that the only acceptable course of action was to overcome all her neurotic difficulties.

Paradoxically, many patients respond to a tenacious questioning of their goals with renewed attempts to achieve developmentally higher goals. The difficulty in achieving these goals based on the influence of others may be because of unacknowledged rebelliousness — success is avoided through the stubborn refusal to yield to another's felt dictates. Sometimes a hidden dependence comes to the surface; so long as the patient adopts the goals of others, he is saved from the work and fantasied dangers of making his own decisions. By exploiting the freedom to make independent, realistic decisions about his life, the patient may achieve a separation and individuation he thought had already been achieved. He may have maintained the fiction of independence through pseudoagreement and compliance with social desires, as if these were his own. And the therapist may have unwittingly added his own desires.

Some therapists may be tempted to pursue developmentally lesser goals as a gimmick like reverse psychology, a pseudo-examination with the goal of achieving an idealized conception of mental health never seriously in question. If such a gimmick works, it will work only briefly. The old situation of extrinsically determined goals, inappropriately yoked with limited capacities or restricted by dependence or rebelliousness, will reassert itself. In order to be successful, the therapist must be sincere in recognizing that only the patient's thorough self-assessment and decisions based on that assessment can succeed in the overall task of settling on and implementing a realizable pattern of life.

Some psychotherapists may be afraid to encourage the patient's free assessment of himself and his settlement on goals that are short of the idealized one. Psychotherapists may worry that they are shortchanging the patient, that their assessments are incorrect, and that the patient may use the setting of inappropriately limited goals as a resistance. Apart from overlooking or misjudging the desirability and workability of resistance, worries about selling the patient short are unnecessary. So long as the psychotherapist adheres to the rules of psychotherapy and so long as he is not simply smuggling in behavior modification under the guise of psychotherapy, the patient will have adequate opportunity to correct any misjudgments.

The therapist's fear itself may indicate his lack of neutrality and mindless pursuit of idealization. He may be afraid that free discussion might influence his patient to decide on goals different from his own. Thus, a discussion of opting for a lesser job might result in the patient's doing just that; a discussion of going to college might result in his not going to college; and a discussion of homosexuality might result in homosexuality. Such fears reveal the therapist's lack of confidence that the truth will set his patient free and suggest the influence of the therapist's bias on his patient. Moreover, if adequate self-examination results in the patient's not going to college, or settling for a lower occupational status, or becoming homosexual, then so be it. Since the patient has to pay the price for what he does in life, he ought to decide what it will be. The psychotherapist has to cope with his or her own disappointment, anxiety, and the assumed reaction of society and his colleagues; that is not the patient's problem.

The patient's problem is to place himself in the passing parade, marching with the group or alone and at the pace and with the style that suits his capacities and direction. Idealizations limit neutrality, curtailed neutrality limits investigation, and restricted investigation limits opportunity. Freely chosen and freely created opportunity is as close to a useful ideal as there is in psychological treatment.

Part IV

Comparing and Evaluating Methods of Change

When an enterprise is engaged in for high stakes, there is a strong likelihood of competitive feelings and actions. People behave as if there is not enough for everyone, and being declared the best carries the promise of continued reward. Such competitive feelings, an expression of insecurity, become exaggerated in the face of fundamental insecurity about the value of what one is doing. Even the best psychotherapists are subject to such feelings. It is in the nature of the calling to deal constantly with tentativeness, hypotheses, and ambiguity, with questions that may or may not have answers at any given moment. So it is understandable that the history of psychotherapy is replete with acrimonious debate about who has the most effective or humane or reasonable brand of psychotherapy. Although great rewards promote such debates, so do scant rewards, when feelings of competition meet head on with shortages of patients or influence or power. I was made especially aware of these issues in the years when I studied the new therapies. When I was with the new therapists, I was challenged by criticisms of psychoanalysts and assertions that what the new therapists were doing was better in one way or the other. When I was with my colleagues, I was challenged to justify my interest in the new therapies, and I was sometimes viewed with the suspicion that I had gone over to the enemy, that I was downgrading psychoanalytic thinking in comparison with the new therapies. So it was, in part, to provide myself with answers and encouragement that I have written this chapter, comparing the psychoanalytic and Gestalt paths to change.

Another way of coping with one's insecurities, and thereby contending with competition, is to do research — the more formal the better — that supports one's point of view. But this means of demonstrating the truth is always rather self-deluding. One has only to notice the many studies that contradict other studies, to listen to debates among acknowledged leaders in the field, and to note how many studies are not replicated or when replicated yield results different from those of the original study. When one relies on scientific findings for self-esteem, one often relies on a weak reed. Research in psychotherapy, even more than research in many other fields, is subject to important criticisms. In Chapter 11, I shall discuss some of the issues that need to be addressed if research in psychotherapy is to demonstrate successfully its validity. Further discussions of the issues in evaluating psychotherapy and comparing the new therapies and conventional psychotherapy are available in my *Out in Inner Space — A Psychotherapist Explores the New Therapies* (1979b).

10
Psychoanalytic and Gestalt Paths to Change

As a psychoanalyst comparing Gestalt therapy and psychotherapies, I am almost sure to write something that either a psychoanalyst or a Gestalt therapist will disclaim as not being the way he does or understands his work. Individual practitioners behave and believe differently from one another, although they nominally practice the same theory and technique.

Another difficulty in discussing psychoanalysis and Gestalt therapy is the sociopsychological nature of our times. The field of psychotherapy has recently become a highly competitive market for men's minds and dollars. In such an atmosphere people tend to lose their identities and become fantasies in the eyes of others; ideas tend to be used as justifications or weapons rather than to be pondered. Psychoanalysis, because of its first and formidable claim to the field, its exclusive training practices, and its identification with the doctor-patient model tends to be seen as the establishment authority against which new ideas must be measured, if not rebelled against. The comparable fantasy about Gestalt therapists is that they are errant younger brothers scrambling for a place in the sun, reckless of the damage done to older institutions, and bolstering their shaky conviction with contempt for orthodoxy. Finally, I as an individual must be included in this list of difficulties. My Gestalt experience consists of the reading of some basic texts, discussions with Gestalt therapists, and observation and participation in a dozen or so Gestalt therapy groups in Los Angeles, Esalen, and Topeka. I have not practiced Gestalt therapy except for using some of its techniques in psychoanalytic therapy. I run the risk, therefore, of misrepresenting and inadequately understanding Gestalt therapy. But if we wait for people to be fully trained and experienced in both psychoanalysis and Gestalt therapy, the comparison of the two will be greatly delayed.

INTERPRETATION

The delivery of insight through interpretation is probably the greatest distinction between Gestalt therapy and psychoanalysis. The extreme Gestalt position would be that no interpretations are made in Gestalt work; indeed no active attempt is made to convey insight. The extreme psychoanalytic position might be that the goal is to convey insight through properly-timed interpretations. Both these positions collapse when one considers interpretation as communication, the goal of which is to enlarge awareness or consciousness. Such a process may include *an* interpretation, that is, an explicit statement of meaning. It also may include any expressive behavior by the therapist which, because of its timing and its interpersonal and intellectual context, can convey emotional and cognitive understanding. Such sources of insight can be silence, matter-of-factness or emotional responsiveness, suppression or encouragement. All can be cues to the meanings the patient can ascribe to his productions. On the basis of my experience, Gestalt therapy will have to be accepted as a highly effective purveyor of insight, however much Gestaltists may dislike being characterized in this way. They cannot have it both ways: to encourage full awareness on the one hand and to claim not to deal in insight on the other. It is true, however, that Gestalt therapists minimize, and some no doubt abstain completely from, explicitly interpretive remarks. Thus, they try not to tell the patient in so many words about himself (although I have seen this done by some esteemed Gestalt therapists along with hortatory, educative, inspirational, and summarizing comments). They do make highly educated guesses about what to emphasize, what roles should be played out in dialogue, what should be repeated louder, and what elements in a dream should be attended to — all under a guiding clinical sophistication, reflecting their own insight or awareness and encouraging the same in the patient.

I think that a better distinction than that between insight and interpretation and no insight and interpretation would be that Gestalt therapists are hypersensitive to the invasion of the interpretive process by emotionally isolated cognition and have designed their techniques accordingly. In Gestalt therapy the patient quickly learns to discriminate between ideas and ideation, between obsessional pathways and new thoughts, and between a statement of experience and a statement of a statement. The Gestalt goal of pursuing experience and not explanations, based on the belief that the insight that emerges as the Gestalt emerges is more potent than the insight given by the therapist, does help the patient and therapist draw and maintain these important distinctions. Psychoanalysts and their patients, on the other hand, have to struggle harder with what seems at times a contradictory attitude toward the pursuit of insight in psychoanalysis, e.g., it is said that those insights that come from the patient himself are best, and yet much of psychoanalytic technique pertains to the analyst's interpretations; insights are held to be most useful when they are accompanied by affect, but interpretations of meaning are not infrequently made with various degrees of emotional involvement.

CAUSE AND CHOICE

Gestalt therapists regularly instruct their patients to substitute "I won't" for "I can't." This small but powerful device is an entry into what in psychoanalysis would be called character analysis. With it the Gestalt therapist implies that he knows that the patient is inclined to minimize his ability and to see his difficulties as external and therefore out of his control. Thus the Gestalt therapist counters any of the patient's inclinations to be stubborn, petulant, or self-defeating. He implies that the patient has the capacity to solve problems, and that if he does not it may well be because he does not want to. Such a point of view is in the traditions of psychoanalytic ego psychology, which posits a capacity for problem solving that is partly independent of and partly an outgrowth of drives, a function of consciousness, will, judgment, decision making, mastery, and self-determination. This view contrasts with the simplistic understanding of behavior as being solely determined by the id, instincts, or unconscious drives and wishes. Freud would never have envisioned a person without choice, driven solely by instincts. The essence of psychoanalysis is internal conflict; the id is opposed by the ego, wishes contend with fears, and impulses compete with each other. To argue against a conflictual view of human nature is to have misunderstood early psychoanalysis and to be ignorant of later psychoanalysis. Such an error is understandable, however; some psychoanalysts sound as if they too believe that drive, wish, and symbolism are all that is important in any given bit of behavior.

Psychoanalysis has had difficulty moving from the discovery and drama of unconscious motives and symbolic meanings to the general psychology intended by Freud. It has remained for systematic innovators, such as Roy Schafer (1968a, 1968b, 1973a, 1973b, 1973c), Allen Wheelis (1950, 1956, 1973), and others to make systematically explicit within psychoanalysis the place of action, reason, will, and decision making as these take place with more or less insight, awareness, and consciousness. Determination in psychoanalysis·is actually multi-determination. Saying that a behavior is unconsciously determined is not the same as saying that it is fully and inexorably determined that way. It merely asserts that unconscious motivation is an influence. In this sense Gestaltists, as they help people see and experience early relationships that are influential in the present, are no less deterministic than are psychoanalysts. They are, however, more explicit, forceful, and perhaps more confident of people's conscious capacities to deal adequately with their troublesomely determined natures.

MEMORY AND THE HERE-AND-NOW

"Talk to your long-dead relative now," "say how you feel now," "act it, be it now," "use the present tense," say the Gestalt therapists in their pursuit of the here-and-now of experience. Their zeal for phenomenology often results in sweeping accusations that sound as if psychoanalytic work consists solely of reconstructing a figurative past on the assumption that this alone will bring about change. This is at best a half-truth, as discussed in a review of McGuire, *Reconstruction in Psychoanalysis* (Appelbaum, 1972). Psychoanalysts and Gestaltists essentially agree that the most mutative experiences are those that involve the whole person, are the most fully experienced, and take place in the present. In psychoanalysis the most powerful tool for achieving these experiences is transference, which by definition is seen most clearly by the patient in the here-and-now of the psychoanalytic hour. Transference duplicates past relationships. Indeed, Freud described transference as a way of remembering. Recalling an event from the past while leaving it there is very different from experiencing the past in the present through the transference. (Even recall, however, can be experienced with its associative feelings, in the present. For example, patients will comment that they had often thought of a particular past event but never "saw" it in the same way as they did when it was recalled during the psychoanalytic hour.) Indeed, a past recreated in the transference may have a greater claim to being in the here-and-now than a past imaginarily re-created in Gestalt role playing and dialogues.

Finally, much of the here-and-now of group behavior and of the relationship with the therapist is ignored by Gestaltists. Gestalt therapists are far less ignorant of the past and its uses than one might gather from some of their comments. For example, a Gestalt therapist might say to a patient, "get into your time machine," as an invitation to remember the past. Their patients do, in fact, usually tell of past experiences that have seemingly been an important determination in the difficulties that they focus on in the Gestalt sessions. Such devices as forcing the patient to use the present do underline the importance of the past as it is presently experienced and thus guard against allowing abstraction and intellectualization to desiccate experience. For the reasons discussed below, Gestalt techniques powerfully evoke emotional awareness of the past as it is experienced in the present.

THE BODY

The importance of the body to personality has as its antecedent in psychoanalysis Freud's understanding that the sense of self is first experienced in bodily terms, which he called the body ego. His theory began in the borderland between the psychological and physical processes to which he was led by his early patients who had bodily symptoms for which no physical cause could be found. He attempted to explain these psychological processes neurologically in *The Project for a Scientific Psychology* (1895a); and although he rejected this model, he hoped that the physicochemical processes underlying these psychological events would eventually be identified. Wilhelm Reich (1949), writing as a traditional though innovative psychoanalyst, suggested that the body not only could express conflict in symptom formation but that the whole configuration of a person's drives and defenses also could be inferred by observing him physically. Ella Freeman Sharpe (1938) believed that the body was a carrier of explicit memories localized in its various parts and that dream imagery often referred to specific bodily experiences of early childhood.

Psychoanalysts have always considered bodily symptoms, posture, gait, and inadvertent movements to express personality. Typically, however, these observations in the psychoanalytic hour are limited to how the patient enters the office, his movements on the couch (as these may be observed by the analyst behind the patient), and how he leaves. Ever since the brief period when Freud attempted to stimulate reverie by putting his hands on the patient's forehead, direct use of the body has been eschewed in psychoanalysis, consistent with Freud's settling on psychophysical parallelism as his solution to the mind-body problem. By contrast, Gestalt therapy emphasizes the opportunities for observing the body, exaggerating its expressiveness, and explicitly manipulating it. Observations are often abetted, especially in Gestalt group sessions, by the patients' opportunities for walking around and finding different positions on the floor. Assuming that the body is a carrier of memory and experience often outside awareness, Gestaltists attempt to release such experience by directly urging the patient to concentrate on his body, to express himself with it, and to change his breathing and body posture; and they often use bioenergetic exercises for these purposes as well.

In summary, psychoanalysis and Gestalt therapy share similar assumptions about the relationship of body to personality, but psychoanalytic technique, through its emphasis on insight, its adoption of psychophysical parallelism, and its standardized physical arrangements, has allowed such ideas to atrophy through their limited use, whereas Gestalt therapy has exploited them.

ACCEPTANCE

Both psychoanalysts and Gestalt therapists assert their nonjudgmental acceptance of the patient. Therefore, they both struggle with the paradox that even while claiming acceptance, they are nonetheless engaged in a procedure that is designed to facilitate change. How this paradox is usually solved by both of them is by merely offering the conditions for change, and it is up to the patient to decide what, when, and how changes should occur. This is probably practical, but it ought not to obscure the recognition that the therapist knows full well that when one goes to a therapist one wants to change something felt to be inimical to his well-being. If the patient were fully accepted by himself and the therapist, there would hardly be any motivation to work; putative patients would just be dilettantes whom no therapy would benefit. The Gestalt therapists, although they often claim the title "therapist," may assert that they are not interested in symptoms and cure, in any goals for the patient except those of increasing awareness, raising consciousness, and encouraging a sense of whole from parts. In contrast, psychoanalytic patients are inclined to present specific symptoms or complaints to the analyst. If they do not do so, most analysts consider it helpful to work toward the patient's recognition of what is alien and unwanted by himself. However, the psychoanalyst might similarly say that he was interested only in making the unconscious conscious, in strengthening the ego, and in the patient's integrating disparate parts of himself. One must distinguish between an atmosphere of nonjudgmental acceptance of the patient and his productions within the treatment and the overall expectation of something better coming of this work which determines whether to embark on it and when to end it. Gestalt therapists are reluctant to acknowledge change as a goal, as if such acknowledgment must lead to a lack of acceptance of the patient's production and his progress at any given moment during the treatment. Some psychoanalysts, because of their medical training and the medical role that they assume politically, socially, and administratively, may have to struggle even more than Gestalt therapists do to maintain this distinction between acceptance in the therapeutic hour and the unacceptability of symptoms and symptomatic behavior. Other psychoanalysts may fall into a routinized, timeless, passive position regarding purposes, life behavior outside treatment, and termination, which are dangers inherent in long-term treatment.

RESISTANCE

The issue of acceptance probably comes up most pointedly in the concept of resistance. Gestalt therapists at times seem to declare resistance unimportant with their exquisite attention to, and premium placed upon, where the patient "is" at the moment. If that "is" does not include an openness to feelings and thoughts and a wish to exploit these, then the patient, at least in group situations, has the option of not "working." He stays off the "hot seat" and may or may not relate to others in the group. Indeed, he may wander entirely out of the situation without his behavior being an object of particular therapeutic interest to anybody. Instead of analyzing resistance, Gestalt therapists assert that the patient needs his resistances, but as a conscious option rather than as an unconscious compulsion. Nonetheless, Gestalt therapists do work with the patient's struggle to be in touch with his thoughts and feelings. Often, they use bodily tonus and stimulation to overcome what a psychoanalyst might call a condition of resistance. For example, they may have the patient attend to his body, breathe deeply, do exercises, get in touch with the lower levels of his mind by acting like primitive people or animals. The Gestalt therapist's seeming disregard for resistance is an effective way of dealing with resistances. For example, he may ask the patient to notice how he is resisting experience and to exaggerate such behavior until the patient feels tired, rueful, found out, or ridiculous at so defeating himself. If the patient resists by waking up before a dream is ended, the therapist may ask, "If you had not awakened, how would the dream have ended?" If the resistance is in the form of not remembering dreams, the therapist may ask, "If you had not forgotten it, what would the dream have been?"

"Going with" the resistance in such ways is a powerful technique. At one stroke the therapist may achieve all or some of the following: neutralizing the patient's stubbornness and negativism by offering him the feeling of independence and control that oppositional people usually crave; recognizing with the patient the need for resistances, thus underlining the therapist's understanding and acceptance; staying out of the potential "countertransference bind" of wanting the patient to go at his own pace but also wanting to move the therapy along; staying out of the transference position of judging behavior as having to be given up as if it were bad; avoiding acting in the paradigm of therapist activity, i.e., getting rid of the resistance, and in the paradigm of patient passivity, i.e., allowing the resistance to be removed, which may be felt by the patient as a deprivation, attack, or loss.

I have been particularly impressed by how much many patients interpret the analyst's interventions as prohibitions and criticisms, no matter how neutrally and nonjudgmentally they are expressed and felt by the psychoanalyst. The psychoanalyst may know that his interventions are functional rather than moral, but the distinction seems difficult for many patients to maintain, and it may not always be easy for the psychoanalyst, either. After all, he does value an intrapsychic situation that is relatively unimpeded by resistances, and he is inclined to describe a patient who can overcome his resistances as a "good" patient, and he does usually select for psychoanalysis only those patients who give evidence of capacities favorable to psychoanalytic success. The Gestalt point of view and consequent feeling about resistances, even apart from the particular techniques used, help minimize any such tendencies toward being judgmental in other than functional ways.

Psychoanalysts usually make resistance the figure without self-consciously attending to the ground of the open, "working" state of consciousness as such; Gestalt therapists make the working state of consciousness the figure, with what are in effect resistant states of mind and consciousness unlabeled as such, though very much attended to. They agree on the nature of resistance, however. The Gestalt emphasis on helping the patient discover "the mechanism by which he alienates part of his self-processes and thereby avoids awareness of himself and environment" (Yontef 1969, p. 217) is a useful definition of resistance.

DREAMS

In psychoanalysis the dream is the guardian of sleep in that it allows partial expression of impulses by symbolically fulfilling the wishes that are psychological expressions of such dammed-up impulses. In Gestalt therapy a dream is described as an existential message from one part of the self to another. On the surface these viewpoints might seem quite different, but in fact the differences are more apparent than real. Even as stated there is nothing necessarily contradictory about these formulations. After all, unfulfilled wishes and their consequences make up most of existence. And there is at least a bit of psychoanalytic lore to the effect that if one traced all the possible associations to any one dream the whole personality would be revealed.

Any seeming differences are even less apparent when one moves from metapsychology to how psychoanalysts use dreams in practice. The dream is not always taken as an actual event of the night, but rather as a communication from the patient to the psychoanalyst in the here-and-now of the psychoanalytic hour. Thus patient and psychoanalyst may learn from when the dream was mentioned, how it was told, and what the patient does with it once it is told. The psychoanalyst may understand the introduction or report of a dream at a particular moment as an avoidance of the here-and-now, or may call attention to it, or he may simply ignore the dream. Or he may react to it as an existential message that the patient, for defensive reasons or because of his lack of conscious awareness, is unable to express in less coded ways. Rather than offering an explanation (which many Gestalt therapists seem to think the psychoanalyst would do), he would probably encourage the patient not only to associate to elements in the dream but also to offer his own understanding. Just as a Gestalt therapist might do, the psychoanalyst might remind the patient that the dream was a creation of the dreamer's mind rather than a representation of people or events apart from himself.

Although both therapists are likely to collect associations

to dream elements, no matter how seemingly irrelevant or unimportant, Gestalt therapists do use a technique not ordinarily used by psychoanalysts—a kind of guided imagery-associative process. This technique is to have the patient become a person or element in the dream and say what comes to mind as this person or element. Proceeding on the belief that everything in the dream reflects aspects of the person, Gestaltists assume that a spoon, window, or coffin can be instructive, just as can such more obvious self-representations as people or animals.

In recent years, the importance of the dream to psychoanalytic technique has diminished to the point that some analysts claim to ignore dreams entirely. It may be that these psychoanalysts have learned that at least their way of using dreams has led to dreams being used more as resistance than as a useful point of entry into the inner life. It seems to me worthwhile for psychoanalysts to explore the Gestalt techniques of role playing with dream elements. By observation and experience I have found that they lead quickly and usefully to emotional experience and insight.

OBJECT RELATIONS VIA DIALOGUE

Constructing a monologue or dialogue based on dream parts is only a variation of the major Gestalt therapy technique of having the patient "play the parts" of himself and people significant in his life. This technique, too, is foreign to psychoanalysis and might well be investigated for its possible effectiveness. Such a procedure dramatizes what the psychoanalyst familiar with object-relations theory might label as the "inner world of objects." It provides dramatic illustrations of the relationships between self and others as these are carried out within the mind of the patient. It demonstrates the interchangeability with and empathy for the people who comprise oneself. Improved self-awareness, and by implication greater tranquility and effectiveness, come about by admitting rather than disowning these "introjects," as one forgives, adjusts to, or otherwise integrates them into a workable, less conflicting whole. Gestaltists work, first, toward recognition of the separateness of introjects, visible by being projected, then toward a reintrojection of them into the self. Such a formulation and way of working would be acceptable to many psychoanalysts, particularly those of Kleinian or other object-relations persuasion.

FREE ASSOCIATION AND "WORKING"

Initially I was surprised at how articulate Gestalt therapy patients were in talking about their problems and difficulties in front of a group. I wondered whether I would be able to "work" adequately on the hot seat. Such fears were unfounded. In a short time I was able to shift gears into a state of consciousness not unlike what one experiences on the psychoanalytic couch, which facilitates free association, openness to experience, and reverie. Maybe the inhibiting effect of a face-to-face confrontation is diminished by the presence of many faces; maybe the atmosphere of acceptance so prevalent in Gestalt work helps one overcome his inhibitions; maybe observing others doing the same thing allows a sense of community that helps allay fear and embarrassment; or maybe impeding the development of a transference relationship is helpful in this regard (see below).

Articulateness and verbal productivity in the Gestalt session seem to stem largely from the free-associative process. Some Gestalt therapists may be surprised at my applying such a term to the flow of ideas when a patient is "working," but I think that this might be a common misunderstanding of the term and phenomena of free association. "Free association" is a misnomer. Associations, by definition, follow rules if not laws. Psychoanalysis posits that associations are determined by motives or impulses and therefore have meaning. What is "free" about the phenomenon is a state of mind that allows thoughts to come, unhampered by judgments as to whether they are moral, intelligent, or important. Freed of such strictures, the patient is helped to allow the rules of determination to operate "freely."

Psychoanalysts make these conditions formal with the basic rule — tell whatever comes to mind — which mostly is only a formality. The atmosphere provided by analysis is enough to encourage the associative process without the rule, just as the Gestalt therapy sessions seem to do. However, the openness of the task denoted by the basic rule is a powerful adjunct to the basic free-associative process, making for wider-ranging associations and also for the emergence of resistances whose analysis becomes central to understanding the personality. By contrast a somewhat more narrative framework, adopted by "working" Gestalt patients, may go deeper and faster, though less broadly. Essentially, however, "working" comes about by letting one thought lead to another, i.e., free associations.

PSYCHOSEXUAL STAGES

Frequently during Gestalt work I found myself translating back and forth between the language of the Gestalt session and the language of psychoanalysis. (At times this procedure served as a resistance; my psychoanalytic self felt slightly guilty and resolved to get back to work. This contrasts with the Gestalt view that such wavering attention indicates a natural wisdom as to how much can be integrated.) An example of this occurred when the issue of intimacy was discussed. The problem of intimacy, according to this Gestalt group leader, was to find a comfortable and effective point between the extremes of "confluence," characterized by the lack of discrimination between people because of a clinging need for others (which might be labeled oral) and excessive distance, a hyperdiscrimination between self and others with rigidly prescribed means of interpersonal contact (which might be labeled anal). The comfortable and effective midpoint between these extremes allows an integration of both of them, to discharge effectively the task of intimacy, and to get the most from and to give the most to relationships (which might be labeled genital).

The Fritz Perls model (1969b) of taking in through the mouth what is compatible and spitting out what is not seems identical with the oral-dependent-oral-aggressive paradigm in psychoanalysis.

CHANGE AND TIME

Gestalt therapists often use what could be labeled corrective emotional experience. They encourage their patients to try out thoughts, expressions, and behaviors to see what feels right for them. They depend on the nonoccurrence of the unconsciously expected consequences as being reassuring to the patient, thereby encouraging him to use these new behaviors and be emboldened to try out still more new ones. This idea seems to underlie "risk taking": "Sure you feel anxious," the Gestalt therapist says, "but don't let that hold you back, try it out, go ahead, and see what happens." Gestaltists do this to increase awareness rather than simply to encourage mindless new behavior, as some therapists do out of a belief that behaving differently in and of itself is sufficient to produce lasting change. The traditional, though not exclusive, psychoanalytic approach is to try to help the patient understand what is making him anxious. With the consequent diminution of anxiety, the patient can proceed with the behavior that has been inhibited by fear. Some psychoanalysts probably are convinced that in all instances insight precedes change, and they consider the patient's action and assertion of will as outside the range of psychoanalytic work. In my opinion, will, action, decision making, and an openness to the possibility that changed behavior can precede and bring about insight are inherent in psychoanalytic thinking, though perhaps they have only recently been fully recognized. The use of understanding, insight, and the psychoanalysis itself as a possible defense against the anxiety of changing one's behavior is, or should be, recognized; as Freud said, sooner or later a phobic patient must face, rather than merely talk about, his phobias (1919). Some psychoanalysts may encourage understanding beyond the point at which accepting extraanalytic challenges should be encouraged (such encouragement can be done analytically, through interpretation, as well as through exhortation). Gestalt therapists probably avoid passivity and intellectualization with their reduced emphasis on insight as an explicit goal and instead their emphasis on the immediate taking of risks, if only in speech during the Gestalt sessions. The danger is that they merely inspire the patient to behave differently, based on suggestion and borrowing the strength of the therapist. Away from the therapeutic influence the changed behavior may well collapse, or the patient may be unable to deal with the consequences of the new behavior.

The Gestalt therapy's attitude toward time is flexible, soft, and maternal: there need never be endings; Gestalt patients may continue attending group or individual sessions indefinitely; and these sessions themselves may go on until their idiosyncratic conclusion. How one feels at the particular moment is all-important, with the understanding that this feeling may change in an instant. The demands of continuity, predictability, beginnings, middles, and ends which are identified with the masculine elements in personality are mostly ignored (Mann 1973). Some patients may find such a point of view reassuring. It lightens the burden of commitments, and it relieves the need for promising and being responsible in the future. Yet the relatively brief time usually allotted to the psychotherapy encourages solving problems quickly.

By contrast, psychoanalysts are rigid about the time boundaries of each session, often make gross predictions of the length of treatment, and are attuned to the psychologies of beginnings, middles, and ends. This scrupulousness about time contradicts the implicit timelessness within the treatment period—what is not dealt with today can be dealt with tomorrow, the wheel comes around again, themes will recur, and four or five years of four or five times a week treatment is unremarkable. For some patients the stipulation of a treatment period may imply that they cannot change their behavior until the treatment has been concluded or has taken effect. The psychoanalyst has to alert himself and the patient to the existence of now, the capacities for self-help that can in principle operate at any given moment. He and the patient must overcome the passivity implicit in waiting and must recognize the illusion that a period of time and treatment, even when it is a long period, can in and of itself result in an improved life ever after.

SELF-SELECTION OF GESTALTISTS
AND PSYCHOANALYSTS

There seems no reason to exempt the choice by practitioners or patients of Gestalt therapy or psychoanalysis from the participation of unconscious motives. Even if there were no Gestalt therapy for middle-aged and older psychoanalysts to choose, the life styles typically practiced by the two groups suggest fundamental differences in their personalities. Gestalt therapists are more informal than psychoanalysts, less inner and goal directed, more direct in their interpersonal relationships, more responsive to the primitive and romantic, and more optimistic, hedonistic, and socialistic. Aggression seems less central to their personalities and to the group atmosphere. The defensive purposes of contrasting life styles of psychoanalysts and Gestaltists probably interfere with their attempts to understand one another's theories and practices for their intrinsic worth. Instead, both groups tend to see each other as caricatures of the inadmissible parts of themselves: the rigid, hyperintellectual, unfeeling, materialistic, traditional psychoanalyst; the sloppy, childlike, fuzzy-faced, fuzzy-minded Gestalt therapist. It is a sad commentary on people who espouse wholeness to split off and project aspects of themselves—sad, but all too human. In principle at least, an integrated psychotherapist could adopt any insights, techniques, emphases, and values to increase his effectiveness. He could do the same with himself as a person. The alternative position would be to convince himself that the way he works achieves the best results possible for all patients, under all circumstances, at the least expense of time and money, and with the least risk—a boldly self-confident position. That he could not improve himself or his life would be, if anything, even more boldly self-confident.

CLOSURE

Both Gestalt therapists and psychoanalysts sound at times as if they have closure as a realizable goal. In Gestalt therapy, the lack of closure is "unfinished business," an unexpressed and unintegrated feeling relative to a person or situation, which by implication at least can be finished. Psychoanalysts set forth goals such as the resolution of the transference, resolution of conflicts, and a complete psychoanalysis. Yet, at the same time both Gestaltists and psychoanalysts also hold as a goal the patient's developing tools with which he can help himself in the future, through self-analysis or through the capacity to make himself increasingly aware. This suggests that neither field considers that its formal treatment efforts provide an absolute solution to the patient's problems. In one systematic research of psychoanalytically oriented psychotherapy and psychoanalysis little conflict resolution was found to have occurred, at least as judged from psychological tests. Other changes in conflicts, such as awareness of them in consciousness, occurred more frequently (Appelbaum 1977a). Reanalysis or further brief analytic work is not uncommon (although Freud's dictum that every person should have further analytic work every five years is honored more in the breach than in the observance.) Gestalt patients often attend continued workshops where they are reminded that what is true for one moment need not be true for the next moment and that determination or ambition for too much change over too long a period of time is inimical to awareness and change ("trying is lying").

"Closure" or "resolution" are most clearly applicable to those moments during the therapeutic work when something is integrated, usually signaled by a feeling of liberation and relief, and the patient is released toward new challenges. It is paradoxical to apply the language of closure—termination, ending, and completion—to the treatment as a whole while at the same time believing that the patient should deal with continuing conflicts in new, perhaps ever changing ways. This is a particular issue for psychoanalysts, who posit comprehensiveness, if not completion, as a purpose and justification for the considerable time and expense of psychoanalysis. Such an implication is realized by the work's having a fixed ending and being offered in the social context of the health-sickness model (inapplicable as that model is to psychoanalysis). In that model, with a prescribed treatment one hopes to cure a sickness definitively.

Gestalt therapists are more flexible in this respect. They are satisfied with fragmentary interventions in regard to the personality and the structure of the treatment. Although some Gestaltists may use a regular schedule of appointments with a fixed ending, others may give patients the option of coming or not coming and when there, of working or not working. This option may open the way for patients' resistances. The patients may keep attending Gestalt workshops and in that way appear to be trying to improve themselves, even without achieving greater awareness; or they may in response to the anxiety of emerging, unintegrated awareness, simply stop attending.

All those who work toward change might benefit from asking themselves whether "closure," "resolution," "completion" are satisfactory words and concepts, whether the human condition permits or admits them. Rather than achieving enduring solutions or lasting joy, the patient, as does any person, has to learn to live with the quest for awareness itself, by recognizing mystery, profundity, and ambiguity of human life and its often ultimately unsatisfactory, and in many ways incomplete, ending.

RELATIONSHIP WITH THE THERAPIST-ANALYST

The following experience is consonant with the Gestalt therapist's attitude toward differentiated interpersonal relationships between patient and therapist:

I had to be late to a Gestalt workshop and therefore missed the new therapist's introduction and preliminary work. Feeling the need to "work," however, I took the hot seat as soon as I could and achieved new insights. I left the workshop not yet knowing the name of the therapist who asked me the right questions, told me the right things to associate to in dreams, interrupted a defensive tangent, made an aspect of my inner world live, and found ways to encourage its intense emotional expression.

For the temporary Gestalt experience, the lack of a differentiated sense of the therapist could be helpful. In the example just cited, I was absorbed with an internal puzzle and in a low-key, unself-conscious way was sufficiently satisfied with what I had seen of the therapist's working with others to be content with knowing what was expected of me and what he would do. The transference characteristics of the therapist, even a "real" relationship with him, could at that moment have been an impediment. If, however, having an extended individual relationship with a benevolent other is important to enduring change, then its absence from Gestalt therapy may be an important loss for some patients. Some psychoanalysts — such as those of the so-called interpersonal school of Sullivan, Will, and Fromm-Reichmann — are much more convinced of and explicit about the curative effects of such relationships than are other psychoanalysts. Whatever the curative effects of the relationship, psychoanalysts focus upon the relationship between patient and psychoanalyst not to practice interpersonal relationships or to provide corrective emotional experience, but as a powerful aid to learning about internal relationships. A transference relationship as a way of learning about oneself is mostly lost to Gestalt patients.

All psychoanalysts are aware that the presence or absence of relationship phenomena can be helpful or harmful, depending upon the situation at the time and the nature and goals of the treatment. It is not a question to be satisfactorily answered for everybody. It does, however, define a psychoanalysis; without a transference relationship the therapy would not be psychoanalysis. This is a major difference between psychoanalysis and Gestalt therapy.

The psychoanalyst is often portrayed as a passive, inscrutable, stone-faced figure sitting in interminable silence. Psychoanalysts use relative passivity, inactivity, and the "active" use of silence so that associations can range widely and deeply. They offer as much neutrality as possible so that the patient can see how he transfers to the analyst other and past relationships. When the Gestalt patient falls into a free-associative state of consciousness, the therapist is highly directive as he circumscribes the general area of association. In place of the patient's relative freedom to let any associations come to mind, the Gestalt therapist directs the patient's productions to some extent. In so doing he decreases the patient's opportunities to react to the therapist in idiosyncratic ways. Also militating against the growth of the relationship between therapist and patient are some Gestaltists' hit-and-miss attitudes toward schedules and toward extended work with only a single therapist.

Gestaltists might profitably ask themselves whether on balance they gain or lose more from minimizing the transference and in being so active. Psychoanalysts might ask themselves if they have perhaps overestimated the amount of injury to the transference and working relationship if they should be more active. Neutrality, after all, is relative; the patient gains much information from how the analyst conducts himself, as well as from what he learns of the analyst outside the hour. If the psychoanalytic base line includes increased activity, and even the use of various active techniques, such behavior may not unmanageably influence the transference and may provide as revealing and useful a base line as the "neutral," traditional one does.

CORRECTIONS FOR PSYCHOANALYSTS AND OTHERS WHOM IT MAY CONCERN

The Gestalt emphasis upon the immediacy of experience, self-responsibility, and mind-body holism could correct for possible errors in psychoanalytic technique. The danger of such technical errors is part of the cost psychoanalysis pays for its elaborate theory whose avowed purpose is to understand all human behavior, motives, adaptations, morals, art, and social groupings. It is a price, too, that psychoanalysis pays for comprising several theories (metapsychological, clinical, experiential, and empirical) which evolved over three-quarters of a century, each generation of analysts learning somewhat different versions. That is a lot of theory to keep in mind, sort out, and select when working with patients. Gestalt practitioners have no such ambitious goals as formulating a science, and their theory is by comparison compact and homogeneous. I do not think that there is anything in Gestalt that is essentially contradictory to the psychoanalytic understanding of personality; with translation, Gestalt would fit comfortably into the commodious psychoanalytic superstructure. That Gestalt techniques differ from those of psychoanalysis, however, gives one pause. People change beneficially as a result of treatment by both kinds of practitioners (and many other kinds of practitioners as well). Such an observation suggests that there are common elements in all these interventions, which patients respond to regardless of the practitioners' language, concepts, and techniques. This is not to say that all interventions are equally successful with all kinds of patients and all kinds of objectives. That involves empirical questions which no one has decisively and definitively answered as yet.

Gestalt techniques were in part designed to counter alleged errors in psychoanalytic technique and theory. Gestalt criticisms can join such revisionist trends in psychoanalysis as dropping the structural and economic points of view and emphasizing phenomenology, process, and experience, all of which have implications for changes in technique. The Gestalt challenge may serve as a helpful stimulus in reraising, in novel ways, issues of flexibility, empathy, concreteness, present–past emphasis, and the capacity and autonomy of the patient, in addition to its offering new techniques for psychoanalysis.

CORRECTIONS FOR GESTALTISTS AND OTHERS
WHOM IT MAY CONCERN

One way psychoanalysts can contribute to Gestalt therapy is to assert the need for an encompassing, differentiated theory of personality on which clinical sophistication and flexibility for differing clinical emergencies can be based. Though for the most part I found Gestalt therapists remarkably sensitive, selecting patient material and techniques which to my mind were responsive to the patient's needs, I have seen instances where I thought a better overall clinical understanding of patients based on theory would have increased the Gestalt therapist's helpfulness.

In one such instance a patient seemed to be complacent about a way of life and kind of self that made others responsible for him and in which aggression was masochistically bound rather than constructively available. In my opinion the therapeutic task and ethical responsibility were to test the limits of his apparent contentment. If he really was without workable or usable conflict, then the therapist should not have interfered with his chosen way of life and in fact could not have changed it anyway. Yet patients may present themselves as satisfied only to respond to diagnostic interventions by becoming anxious and aware that they wish they could live and feel differently. In this instance one such intervention could have been to confront the patient with why he was participating in the Gestalt workshop. But such an intervention could not have been made when a perfectly acceptable reason for being there was simply to "enlarge awareness" or to "raise consciousness." As with any jargon, such phrases can obscure motives and deflect potentially unsettling intrusions. Moreover, as I found out, such confrontations were alien to the spirit of the therapy group and fell on unreceptive ears. This patient may go from one Gestalt therapy group to another, increasing his awareness and raising his consciousness without ever coming to terms with the conflicts that I suspect are depriving him of a choice as to his way of life.

In another example, a woman portrayed herself as not being

able to find a man who could provide her with as much joy as did her lover in the occasional moment when he had time for her. The therapist seemed to accept at face value that no other man in the world could satisfy her, ignoring the information that when she was not available, her lover's interest in her increased. In my opinion her need for such a sadomasochistic relationship was preventing her from finding other kinds of gratification. To suggest, as was done, that for her the task was simply to decide whether or not her joy in this relationship was sufficient and to proceed accordingly, could help spell the end to her stated hopes for marriage and motherhood.

Even if my judgments in these examples are correct, they hardly prove anything. A Gestalt therapist, indeed another psychoanalytic clinician, could find in the caseloads of any psychoanalyst "mistakes" of one kind or another. I cite the examples only to illustrate how training rooted in an understanding of psychopathology is necessary to guide clinical actions and decisions.

I am concerned, also, about the casual attitude of some Gestalt workers toward shaky ego functioning — the possibility of injuring the patient by encouraging more psychological work than the patient can master. This attitude may stem from an inability to assess such dangers, often difficult for anyone no matter how well trained, which sometimes requires hours of psychological testing. It is often explained by Gestaltists as being based on the belief that the patient should be given credit for the ability to maintain himself. I think there are probably instances in which psychoanalytic clinicians might step in with support too soon, minimizing the patient's capacity to help himself. I think it just as likely that there are instances in which the patients cannot sufficiently help themselves and, if unsupported, needlessly develop symptoms, act on the environment in harmful ways, commit suicide, or become psychotic. I saw no such instances myself; indeed, I saw a Gestalt therapist deal effectively with one such danger by unwinding the patient from an emotional pitch that threatened to get out of hand, primarily through helping the patient anchor himself in his bodily experiences. I do think, however, that some patients, if subjected to Gestalt work without interpersonal or environmental supportive measures being available, would risk being harmed. Deciding if, when, and how such measures should be used seems to me to require a comprehensively trained clinician with many interpersonal or environmental options available.

Such clinical mistakes should hardly be surprising. Gestalt therapists say that they are in favor of systematically training practitioners, and compared to some new brands of psychotherapy, they do have extensive training and high standards. However, compared to that of psychoanalysis, the training of Gestalt therapists is limited, being shorter, less systematic, and providing less clinical experience. I am less surprised at seeing what I considered to be clinical errors than that I saw so few. Without adequate comparative studies, we are left with questions about the usefulness for treating patients of the therapist's familiarity with developmental theory, general psychology, the differing psychologies of men and women, psychopathology, and other aspects of conventional training. But this cannot be resolved without also settling problems of differing goals of the practitioner and the different capacities and wishes of the patient. Training has to be commensurate with task, although to ascertain what a particular therapeutic task should be itself requires considerable expertise.

A VIEW FROM ABOVE

We may ask ourselves how the overall system, the culture, and our world are being served by the emergence of Gestalt therapy and the many other therapies that have developed in recent years. We are encouraged to take this perspective because these therapies seem part of a cultural revolution; they are not just technical or scientific emendations and discoveries. One not only practices Gestalt therapy instead of psychoanalysis but often does it without shoes, using first names and resting on psychedelically inspired pillows, while disregarding

time boundaries, being nourished by organic food, spurning
material possessions and Western culture, and admiring absten-
tion and Eastern philosophy. In short, Gestalt therapy is crest-
ing a wave of frustration and revolt, of regret for the past,
distrust of the present, and pessimism about the future, while at
the same time formulating an optimistic response with ancient
antedecents. The current generation of world citizens is the first
to have been born into a world in which the possibility of mass
death from nuclear destruction is always present. Rather than
being unduly fanciful, it seems parsimonious and hardheaded to
me to understand the current resentment of how we got here
and the determination that the future will be different in accordance with this atmosphere of imminent extinction.

Psychoanalysis began as an intellectual rebellion, as a decisive new chapter in Western man's thoughts about his nature
and his world. But through its association with science and
materialism and emphasis upon reason, psychoanalysis has
come to be seen as a social and administrative arm of the Western establishment and is legally and socially sanctioned by it. As
such, many feel it should be opposed. In principle, this should
not matter. The substance of psychoanalysis still remains a
powerful means of systematically understanding all of human
nature. Psychoanalysis still offers the freedom of being able to
think all of one's thoughts and liberate all of one's behavior from
unknown constraints. Psychoanalysis is itself always rebelling
against much of what is wrong in our culture. Unfortunately,
many workers in the field of human change have only sparse
knowledge of psychoanalysis, and they confuse its social and
legal position with its substance. In large part psychoanalysis
has only itself to blame for this. Its exclusive training practices
have made it impossible for many people interested in and capable
of working with the human condition to learn psychoanalysis.
That such people should find a new path, perhaps in part founded
upon resentment of this exclusion, is hardly surprising.

From a general point of view Gestalt and the other new therapies have been used to bring about corrections, additions, and
emphases beneficial to all the sciences of human improvement

and change. The human mind, scientific or otherwise, is dialectical and polarizing. In sharp contrast to the "activity" of a traditional medical practitioner at the turn of the century, Freud discovered that "passivity" allowed the emergence of information about the mind. Psychoanalysis is now identified with passivity and may indeed be too much so. The same criticism of overemphasis could be leveled against such psychoanalytic discoveries as the importance of unconscious motivation and the influence of the past on the present. Within psychoanalysis the dialectical pendulum has been swinging back toward a more balanced view as analysts become more active, as they take multi-determination more seriously, and as they recognize the implications of autonomous ego functions, neutralized drives, manifest dream content, and the power of consciousness. Further reflection and corrections are implicitly being offered by Gestalt therapy, among others, as part of the overall scientific system that embraces and is responsible for the development of all thought. If any of us are to benefit from the ideas and experiences of others, then the whole has to be defined not as psychoanalysis alone, nor as Gestalt therapy alone, but as knowledge.

11

Questioning the Effectiveness of Change in Psychotherapy

How does one assess the effectiveness of psychotherapy? One test of effectiveness is popularity, and increasingly psychotherapy seems to be accepted as part of our culture. This may be so because of people's needs and hopes for improvement, which have led people throughout the ages to believe in a system of thought or activity that promises to make life better. Some therapy or growth experiences seem, at least temporarily, to help people overcome their loneliness, to offer emotional peaks, and to be refreshing and fun. Some people value their psychotherapy because of a need to believe they have spent their time and money wisely or out of their good feelings toward the therapist.

Another measure of the effectiveness of psychotherapy is in the individual clinician's case examples, which portray what is accomplished. An implicit validity lies in our noticing that valued teachers spend their lives in the activity of psychotherapy and consider it worthwhile to teach. Though learning by authority has been criticized as Western civilization has come to believe that truth is learned through the scientific method, most learning in fact takes place through authority. This is true whether the authority resides in an individual known to the student or whether it adheres to the printed word.

Formal research on whether or not psychotherapy is effective has, on the whole, been unconvincing. Some studies show that untreated patients do as well over a period of time as treated ones, and vice versa; that patients improve, remain the same, and get worse no matter what interventions they are subjected to; that the training of the therapist produces better results, that the therapist's training does not matter; and that therapy is based on dynamic principles is more effective than that based on learning theory, and vice versa.

Contradictory research findings are not the only reason why one should question the effectiveness of psychotherapy. If one considers the problems inherent in such research, it become difficult to believe that there could be definitive and consistent answers.

The first of these problems lies in the patient. Unfortunately, in most research, there is no such thing as *the* patient, there is only *a* patient, not like any other. Psychotherapy is an intensely idiosyncratic enterprise to which different people can be expected to react in different ways. If discussed at all, this problem is typically answered by means of diagnostic categories. This is usually unsatisfactory for two reasons. One is the lack of homogeneity in methods of diagnosis. Some people rely exclusively on diagnostic interviews, and others use psychological testing — sometimes group testing and sometimes individual testing, often with different tests and with examiners of differing levels of training and theoretical orientation. There is little agreement on what is meant by the various diagnostic categories. For example, what is called schizophrenia in one country, or part of one country, is not called schizophrenia in another. And observations of the same patient by different clinicians can produce different diagnoses. The second reason is that even if diagnostic categories are homogeneous and reliable, the questions often asked about the effectiveness of psychotherapy are too refined to be answered by such gross categorization. People within diagnostic categories can still be expected to vary widely in relevant respects. Their ego strength, anxiety tolerance, qualities of interpersonal relationships, and psychological-mindedness, as examples, account for considerable differences in the nature and extent of the effectiveness of the psychotherapy. The question of the effectiveness of psychotherapy requires the further specification of effectiveness for *whom*, and that "whom" is a combination of many characteristics.

Just as patients vary widely as individuals, so too do therapists. In many psychotherapies the personality of the therapist is as significant a variable as his theory and his technique. In many studies, this variable is usually ignored, as is the level of the therapist's training. In other studies therapists are categorized as "experienced" or "inexperienced." In the Psychotherapy Research Project of the Menninger Foundation the criterion for "experience" was considered to be at least two years beyond the residency. Such a categorization is probably only a slight improvement over entirely ignoring the therapists' individual differences. The kind and quality of training of psychotherapists vary so extensively that the number of years of training as a measure of skill, or as a means of equating therapists, is all but meaningless. Even if training were homogeneous, individual differences in skill would likely erode the effects of small differences in years of training.

Finally, one must add to the various sources of individual differences among patients and therapists the match between them. People who assign patients to therapists have long been at least informally aware of the effects of such matches. As noted earlier, the research on the effects of marriage and friendship relationships between partners of varying sibling positions, for example, suggests that therapist and patient relationships may be influenced by sibling position as well (Toman 1976).

Much psychotherapy research errs in using experimental designs that are modeled on the testing for effectiveness of medicines. Psychotherapy is not like aspirin, a homogeneous product to be dispensed in a standard way. The psychotherapeutic transaction is unique, taking place in a particular way between a particular patient and a particular therapist, and only once.

The outcome of psychotherapy has also been treated in much psychotherapy research as analogous to the outcome of conventional medical treatments: the patient is determined to have an illness that is judged to have remained the same, gotten worse, or improved to some degree. In such a model there is an implicit assumption that the best one can hope for is that the patient has returned to his premorbid functioning. This is inapplicable to much psychotherapy. The complaint, symptom, or whatever passes for illness that ostensibly brought the patient to treatment often turns out to be more a ticket of admission than the main focus and goal of psychotherapy. True, there are instances of specific symptom complaints that can be judged as worsening, improving, or being removed. Usually, however, the beginning symptom or complaint gives way to hope for change in the patient's way of life or quality of life, in his self-knowledge, feelings about himself, his relationships with others, and in his effectiveness in various life tasks. Judgments of this kind are extremely difficult to make, not only at the end of treatment but also at the baseline when one is dependent upon history or retrospection. Such judgments may differ when made from the points of view of the patient, of society, of the therapist, or of the researcher. Each may have his own set of values, wishes, and means of making comparisons and judgments. For example, a patient may give up an alloplastic behavior to the delight of the environment. But cut off from this way of managing anxiety, he may feel greater distress than he did before. Or the patient may increase his self-esteem by being able to stand up for his own rights, much to the dismay of those in the environment who have benefited from his submissiveness. The patient may be happy with a life plan that, to the therapist, is a compromise significantly below what the therapist expects could have been possible had the patient been able to resolve or work through conflicts in a better way.

Research on outcome would be more useful if treatment goals were considered separate from life goals. Treatment goals are to overcome symptoms and impediments to continued lines of development within a pattern, whereas life goals are those pertaining to the way and quality of life as a total and perhaps changed pattern over time. Psychotherapy may bring improvement in one but not the other.

At what time does one measure the effectiveness of psychotherapy? Usually, this is done at the termination of the treatment.
But there are good reasons to believe that this is an unfortunate
time, since the termination of psychotherapy is, almost by
definition, a special and stressful moment. At termination some
patients tend to exaggerate their gains, out of gratitude to the
therapist and out of a need to justify their investment. Other
patients are inclined to minimize their gains out of resentment at
having the treatment brought to an end and out of disappointment that their fantasied wishes are now seen as irrevocably
beyond them. Even without the artifacts introduced by the factor of the termination itself, the attainment of certain goals
cannot be judged until some time after the end of therapy. Especially with respect to life goals, the psychotherapy may be a
beginning rather than an ending, making it possible for the
patient to meet challenges which before the psychotherapy
seemed beyond his capabilities. To the extent that the effectiveness of the psychotherapy is measured by the quality and nature of
life, the time to assess these goals is not at the end of treatment,
but at the end of life. Few research designs include even temporally modest follow-up assessments. Yet some follow-up assessments show substantial change from the time of termination
(Appelbaum 1975).

In probably no other body of research is the independent
variable less homogeneous and specifiable than in research on
the effectiveness of psychotherapy. It is almost embarrassing to
notice that what is called "psychotherapy" may take place in
such periods of time as four days to four years. It may refer to a
remarkably large number of diverse techniques based upon
remarkably diverse theories of personality. And change may be
brought about by factors not specified in theory or self-
consciously employed in practice. Even granting a similarity of
names or theories or approximate styles and techniques of intervention, it is very difficult to be confident that, in fact, what is
actually done by all practitioners fits the name given to it. Even
psychoanalysis, whose basic model is among the most uniform
and homogeneous of treatments, was likened by Freud to a
chess game in which the beginning and ending moves could be

known, while the rest were subject to innumerable variations. This is probably even more true now as the range of technical problems and kinds of patients treated with psychoanalysis has widened since the basic model was set forth with respect to hysterics—a kind of patient rarely seen nowadays in most psychiatric centers.

All of the difficulties in doing research on psychotherapy noted thus far could be subsumed under the problem of individual differences. For the researcher, these limit the validity and generalizability of his findings. For the prospective patient, they imply that with respect to his particular decision as to whether or not to have therapy, there is little precedent by which to be guided. One may ask, then, what the value is of attempting to do research on psychotherapy if psychotherapy is a scientifically unwieldy enterprise with limited practical value for a particular prospective patient.

The main potential value, it seems to me, is investigating how people change. Ordinarily, such investigation precedes the question of effectiveness—observation comes first, which leads to the specification of the independent variable and its relationships. This stage of research has been somewhat slighted in the research on psychotherapy because psychological research is modeled on medical research, which in turn is sometimes modeled on research in the physical sciences. A consequence of modeling psychological research on medical research was the pragmatic drive to see whether psychotherapy worked, to some extent slighting the careful, delineated knowledge of what psychotherapy substantively was. This drive also led to the assumption that the distinctions among psychotherapies accounted for most of the observed differences. Thus, most researchers in psychotherapy over the last two decades categorized psychotherapy as individual or group (according to orthodox Freudian principles or those of so-called deviant psychoanalysts), as psychoanalysis or psychotherapy, or as dynamic versus client-centered psychotherapy. In recent years, however, the knowledge of how people change and how this is done has expanded greatly. This knowledge has been gained within psychoanalytic psychotherapy through increased thought about the process of change, and outside psychoanalytic psychotherapy by the new therapies founded upon the recognition of new or newly emphasized variables in the process of change. Throughout this book, and especially in Chapter 1, I have discussed elements likely to be relevant to change in psychotherapy — insight, interpersonal relationships, suggestion, expression of emotions, emphasis on will, action, and the power of consciousness.

In the ideal research design the contributions of the different ways people may change would be assessed according to the kinds of interventions made, the structural arrangements, and the theory. And all of this would be subject to the variations introduced by different patients and different outcomes that the interventions produce. These are rigorous, if not utopian, requirements. For formal research in psychotherapy, we shall have to be content now with partial and suggestive answers.

Perhaps, in the recent decades of enthusiasm for formal scientific methods as applied to behavioral science, with its implicit overconfidence, if not worship of technology as a panacea, we may have overlooked simpler ways of providing at least modest answers. We may have overlooked our skills as clinicians as applied to research. If, indeed, generalization and validity are so difficult to determine because of the uniqueness of each psychotherapeutic endeavor, then the examination of single cases may be the research design appropriate to the problem. Such examinations may make it possible to include, and perhaps to control, a greater number of the possibly relevant variables than would be possible in designs involving groups of patients. There are many ways in which clinicians, working with single cases, can systematize and collect their observations. For example, it could become regular practice to have patients tested before and after treatment. It could be a regular practice for therapists to assess the results of diagnostic examinations or the notes of the therapy at periodic intervals as well as at termination. It could become a regular practice for patients to be seen some time after the completion of treatment, long enough afterward so as to be minimally influenced by the termination process and routine enough so that the invitation would not be viewed as a continuation of the relationship. In short, much more can be done with the case history method than is usually done.

Many psychotherapists, it seems to me, have been intimidated by the aura and paraphernalia of formal research, to the point that an unnecessarily wide schism has developed between clinicians and researchers. Such workers seemed to have forgotten a lonely clinician at the turn of the century named Freud, who saw his patients until 9:00 in the evening, then systematized his observations in writing as a research scientist for several hours after that. In addition to the attitudes of physician and humanitarian, he brought from the laboratory to the armchair a research attitude. And what is a research attitude? Surely included would be logic and systematic thinking in general. Superseding even these would be the wish to know — zest, enthusiasm, curiosity, and a sense of adventure in the pursuit of knowledge. I am inclined to think that these characteristics can be found in many clinicians who have not yet identified themselves as researchers.

The final answer to the question of the effectiveness of psychotherapy may always be just beyond our finger tips. But the quest for that answer can be shared by many of us, and in the process we will likely enrich our capacities to bring about change.

Epilogue

There have been three themes in the preceding pages that together unify the otherwise disparate aspects of effecting change in psychotherapy. These themes are the relationships among (1) psychoanalysis and psycho- therapy, (2) conventional psychotherapy including psychoanalysis and the new therapies, and (3) general and specific factors in the process of change.

The thesis of this discussion requires the following recognitions and beliefs: When people meet regularly under relatively unstructured conditions with the goal of self-understanding, their experience will be influenced by past experiences with significant other people; they will react to the work of self-understanding with behaviors designed to impede that work; their behavior in that sit- uation and everywhere else is influenced by thoughts and feelings more or less outside their awareness; and these thoughts and feelings have their inception in early child- hood. All these influences, i.e., transference, resistance, the unconscious, and influence of the past on the present, are available as powerful means of self-understanding. When one participant lies on a couch and the other sits out of sight, each participant is aided in listening, attending to, and producing thoughts and feelings. Finally, the more that the process incorporating all of these and other elements is guided by the clinical theory of psychoanalysis (developmental, dynamic, and the differing psychologies of men and women), the more clearly this behavior can be understood.

Although at first it may appear so, I am not asserting unequivocally that psychoanalysis has the best chance of producing beneficial change. As I have said throughout this book, statements about psychotherapy have limited generality, and this generality is often restricted by the different circumstances of each psychotherapy—no two psychotherapies are alike, just as no two people are alike, and these differences are usually crucial. I do assert that when patient, psychoanalyst, and circumstances meet certain criteria, psychoanalysis then has the greatest chance for effecting beneficial change. Conversely, under different circumstances, with different patients, and with different psychoanalysts, psychoanalysis may not only be inferior to other kinds of treatments but disastrous. In general, however, those psychotherapies that most fully exploit the main psychoanalytic elements of beneficial change have the best chance of success. Or, according to the aphorism, every treatment should be as expressive as possible. Psychotherapy, then, is a procedure that deviates from the fullest exploitation of the central elements of beneficial change as circumstances require, but optimally does so only as little as such circumstances require. The same can be said for junctures within psychoanalysis which, though they are the vehicle for fully exploiting these elements of change, may also encounter circumstances that dictate deviations.

The new therapies' relationship to conventional psychotherapy can be conceptualized as being similar to the one just described between psychoanalysis and psychotherapy: To what extent can the beliefs and practices of the new therapies contribute to the exploitation of the main psychoanalytic elements of beneficial change? Primal screaming and the Gestalt therapist's use of dialogues with "persons" in an empty chair can be used to infuse the sessions with emotion, and also to help summon thoughts and feelings outside awareness. The overcoming of resistances can be aided by the body therapies, an application of Reich's assertion that psychological resistance has become encapsulated in the body as "character armor" and that techniques of breathing as well as exercises and manipulations can break up such resistant armor. The new therapists' emphasis on self-responsibility can be seen both as a way of focusing attention on the ego, its executive functions of action and decision, and as an implementation of the quest for insight and for transforming insight into gross behavioral change. The new therapists offer correctives, reminders, and emphases that can improve psychoanalytic technique. Their emphasis on the present may interrupt any undue preoccupation with the past and in general highlights the issue of whether material from past, present, or transference is being ignored or used as a defense against material from other sources. Similarly, the structural arrangements of the new therapies can increase the effectiveness of psychoanalytic technique, for example, longer marathon sessions or live-in therapies, as are already practiced in hospital milieus organized along psychoanalytic principles. The new therapists' emphasis on action may interrupt any unwarranted passivity; the new therapists' neutrality may protect against any encouragement of inhibitions or limitations of choice founded on insidious morality or unrecognized prejudices. The new therapists' attitudes toward and practices of selection and training may encourage practitioners of conventional psychotherapy to review and perhaps change their means of selection and training. The new therapists' rejection of the analogy between psychological treatment and medical treatment may supply a welcome corrective to any unnecessary emphasis on pathology, thus highlighting the often existential goals of psychotherapy and the need for creation rather than adjustment.

All these may help to improve the effectiveness of producing change by means of psychoanalytic principles. In that respect they are similar to, for example, the use of dreams. Conceivably, psychoanalysis could have been developed independent of the analysis of dreams (and some psychoanalysts even now, deplorably, minimize the use of dreams). In that fanciful circumstance, the analysis of dreams might have been seen as a gimmick much as primal screaming or the empty-chair dialogue is now seen. Dreams would then have had to prove their usefulness to psychoanalysis, probably despite the skepticism at their being a deviation. Whether, how, and to what extent any new therapists' beliefs and practices might be adopted is dependent upon research and experience. To be successful, research and experience should not be hampered by undue, sometimes ritualistic fears of interfering with standard psychoanalytic processes. Such interference, as with any intervention, requires and offers an opportunity for understanding of its meaning. Thus, interpretation itself can be considered an interference — it interrupts free associations and may diminish some sources of curiosity — and requires analysis of how it is experienced and used.

When noting nonspecific factors in psychotherapy, some people develop a kind of nihilism regarding the central elements of beneficial psychotherapeutic change.

They may believe that it does not matter what the participants talk about so long as they do so in a psychotherapeutic atmosphere and under the auspices of a psychotherapeutic stance that allows non-specific factors free play. Such a point of view is not only unreasonably nihilistic but also is simplistic. All factors of change, specific and non-specific, can be ranked according to their mutative capacities. Such capacities will vary from time to time within any psychotherapy. Sometimes expression of feeling will be the most helpful, at other times the interpersonal relationship will, and under some circumstances the treatment will depend on the use of suggestion. There may be clinical situations in which non-specific elements are all that is necessary for beneficial change. In other situations these elements may be, or may become, largely irrelevant. Rather than recognizing non-specific factors as replacements of others, they might better be considered as additions.

I have attempted in this book to emphasize those factors that produce the most effective beneficial change in psychotherapy. By so doing I hope to counteract any rigidities or narrowness of vision that may have prevented some factors from being considered, experimented with, and ultimately used. As I noted in earlier chapters, it is fashionable in some circles to ascribe the unwillingness to consider all points of view as characteristic of psychoanalytic psychotherapists, especially psychoanalysts. But this same unwillingness can be applied to the revisionists within conventional psychotherapy and to the new therapists also. Because of socio-psychological influences and varied training, as well as unconscious resistance, the potential effectiveness and applicability of the main psychoanalytic elements of psychotherapeutic change are often underestimated. In my opinion the aphorism holds: every psychotherapy should be as expressive as possible. All efforts should be made to use fully the main psychoanalytic elements of beneficial change in psychotherapy, however unconventional these efforts may at first appear. Wisdom borne of experience, rather than prejudice born of ignorance, should dictate both adherence to and deviations from Freud's beliefs and techniques.

References

Abraham, K. (1953). A particular form of neurotic resistance against psychoanalytic method. *Selected Papers of Karl Abraham, M.D.,* trans. D. Bryan and A. Strachey. New York: Basic Books.

Aichhorn, A. (1945). *Wayward Youth.* New York: Viking.

Alexander, F. (1946). The principle of corrective emotional experience. In *Psychoanalytic Therapy* by F. Alexander and T. M. French. New York: Ronald.

Alexander, F., and French, T. M. (1946). *Psychoanalytic Theory: Principles and Application.* New York: Ronald.

Allport, G. (1961). *Pattern and Growth in Personality.* New York: Holt, Rinehart and Winston.

Appelbaum, S. A. (1961). The end of the test as a determinant of responses. *Bulletin of the Menninger Clinic* 25:120–128.

——(1963). The pleasure and reality principles in group process teaching. *British Journal of Medical Psychology* 36:49–56.

——(1966a). The Kennedy assassination and the oedipal struggles of a training group. *Psychoanalytic Review* 53:393–404.

——(1966b). Speaking with the second voice: evocativeness. *Journal of the American Psychoanalytic Association* 14:462–477.

——(1967). The world in need of a leader: an application of group psychology to international relations. *British Journal of Medical Psychology* 40:381–392.

——(1969). Psychological testing for the psychotherapist. *Dynamic Psychiatry* 2:158–163.

————(1970). Science and persuasion in the psychological test report. *Journal of Consulting and Clinical Psychology* 35:349–355.

————(1972). Did it really happen? Book review of *Reconstructions in Psychoanalysis* by Michael T. McGuire, in *Psychotherapy and Social Science Review* 7:24–27.

————(1973a). Psychological-mindedness: word, concept, and essence. *International Journal of Psycho-Analysis* 54:35–46.

————(1973b). Self-help with diagnosis: A self-administered semi-projective device. *Journal of Projective Techniques and Personality Assessment* 39:349–359.

————(1975a). The idealization of insight. *International Journal of Psychoanalytic Psychotherapy* 4:272–302.

————(1975b). Parkinson's law in psychotherapy. *International Journal of Psychoanalytic Psychotherapy* 4:426–436.

————(1975c). Questioning the question: what is the effectiveness of psychotherapy? *Inter-American Journal of Psychology* 1–2:213–252.

————(1976). A psychoanalyst looks at Gestalt therapy. In *The Handbook of Gestalt Therapy*, ed. C. Hatcher and P. Himelstein. New York: Jason Aronson.

————(1977a). *The Anatomy of Change: A Menninger Foundation Report on Testing the Effects of Psychotherapy*. New York: Plenum.

————(1977b). The refusal to take one's medicine. *Bulletin of the Menninger Clinic* 41:511–521.

————(1978). Pathways to change in psychoanalytic therapy. *Bulletin of the Menninger Clinic* 42:239–251.

————(1979a). The dangerous edge of insight. *Psychotherapy, Theory, Research, and Practice* 16:364–370.

————(1979b). *Out in Inner Space — A Psychoanalyst Explores the New Therapies*. New York: Doubleday/Anchor.

Appelbaum, S. A., and Holzman, P. S. (1962). The color-shading response and suicide. *Journal of Projective Techniques* 26:155–161.

————(1967). End-setting as a therapeutic event. *Psychiatry* 30:276–282.

Balint, M., Ornstein, P. H., and Balint, E. (1972). *Focal Psychotherapy*. London: Tavistock.

Bartley, W. W., III. (1978). *Werner Erhard, the Transformation of a Man: The Founder of est.* New York: Clarkson N. Potter.

Beres, D. (1957). Communication in psychoanalysis and in the creative process: a parallel. *Journal of the American Psychoanalytic Association* 5:408–423.

Bibring, E. (1954). Psychoanalysis and the dynamic psychotherapies. *Journal of the American Psychoanalytic Association* 2:745–770.

Bird, B. (1957). The curse of insight. *Bulletin of the Philadelphia Association for Psychoanalysis* 7:101–104.

Birdwhistell, R. J. (1959). Contributions of linguistic-kinesic studies to the understanding of schizophrenia. In *Schizophrenia*, ed. A. Auerback. New York: Ronald.

Blanck, G., and Blanck, R. (1974). *Ego Psychology: Theory and Practice.* New York: Columbia University Press.

Breuer, J., and Freud, S. (1895). *Studies on Hysteria*, trans. and ed. J. Strachey. New York: Basic Books, 1957.

Burnham, D. (1974). The influence of theoretical models on the treatment of schizophrenia, reported by J. L. Gunderson. *Journal of the American Psychoanalytic Association* 22:182–199.

Butler, J. (1962). On the naturalistic definition of variables: an analogue of clinical analysis. *Research in Psychotherapy* 2:178–205.

Cassirer, E. (1946). *Language and Myth.* New York: Harper.

Charny, I. W. (1975). The psychotherapies and encounters of the seventies: progress or fads? *Reflections* 10(3):1–17.

Dass, R. (1976). *The Only Dance There Is.* New York: Jason Aronson.

Dewald, P. A. (1965). Reactions to the forced termination of therapy. *Psychiatric Quarterly* 39:102–126.

———(1966). Forced termination of psychoanalysis. *Bulletin of the Menninger Clinic* 30:98–110.

Diatkine, R. (1968). Indications and contraindications for psychoanalytic treatment. *International Journal of Psycho-Analysis* 49:266–270.

Eissler, K. R. (1953). Ego structure and analytic technique. *Journal of the American Psychoanalytic Association*, 104–143.

———(1963). Notes on the psychoanalytic concept of cure. *Psychoanalytic Study of the Child* 18:424–463.

————(1965). *Medical Orthodoxy and the Future of Psychoanalysis.* New York: International Universities Press.

————(1969). Irreverent remarks about the present and the future of psychoanalysis. *International Journal of Psycho-Analysis* 50: 461–471.

Ekstein, R. (1950). The tower of Babel in psychology and psychiatry. *American Imago* 7:76–141.

————(1956). Psychoanalytic technique. In *Progress in Clinical Psychology,* ed. D. Brower and L. E. Abt. New York: Grune and Stratton.

————(1959). Thoughts concerning the nature of the interpretive process. In *Readings in Psychoanalytic Psychology,* ed. M. Levitt. New York: Appleton-Century-Crofts.

Erikson, E. H. (1951). Jewish character traits. In *Christians and Jews* by R. M. Loewenstein. New York: International Universities Press.

————(1953). Growth and crises of the "healthy personality." In *Personality in Nature, Society and Culture,* ed. C. Kluckholm, H. A. Murray, and D. M. Schneider. New York: Knopf.

————(1964). *Insight and Responsibility.* New York: W. W. Norton and Co., Inc.

Fenichel, O. (1941). *Problems of Psychoanalytic Technique.* New York: Psychoanalytic Quarterly, Inc.

————(1945). *The Psychoanalytic Theory of Neurosis.* New York: W. W. Norton and Co., Inc.

————(1954). Brief psychotherapy. In *Collected Papers of Otto Fenichel,* 2nd series. New York: W. W. Norton and Co., Inc.

Ferenczi, S. (1955). *The Selected Papers of Sandor Ferenczi,* ed. M. Balint. New York: Basic Books.

Fiedler, L. (1968). Remark made at symposium: the role of norms in the definition of the national interest. Center for International Studies, New York University, New York.

Frank, J. D. (1971). Therapeutic factors in psychotherapy. *American Journal of Psychotherapy* 25:350–361.

————(1974). Psychotherapy: the restoration of morale. *American Journal of Psychiatry* 131(3):271.

Freud, A. (1954). The widening scope of indications for psychoanalysis. *Journal of the American Psychiatric Association* 2:607–620.

Freud, S. (1895a). The project for a scientific psychology. *Standard Edition* 1:283–297. London: Hogarth, 1966.

———(1895b). Studies on hysteria. *Standard Edition* 2:1–319. London: Hogarth, 1955.

———(1905). On psychotherapy. *Standard Edition* 7:255–268. London: Hogarth, 1953.

———(1908). Creative writers and day-dreaming. *Standard Edition* 9:141–153. London: Hogarth, 1958.

———(1909). Analysis of a phobia in a five-year-old boy. *Standard Edition* 10:3–149.

———(1912). Recommendations for physicians on the psychoanalytic method. *Standard Edition* 12:109–120. London: Hogarth, 1958.

———(1913). Further recommendations in the technique of psycho-analysis, I. *Standard Edition* 12:121–144. London: Hogarth, 1958.

———(1914). On the history of the psychoanalytic movement. *Standard Edition* 14:3–66. London: Hogarth, 1957.

———(1916–1917). Introductory lectures on psychoanalysis. *Standard Edition* 16:347. London: Hogarth, 1968.

———(1917). Mourning and melancholia. *Standard Edition* 14:239–260. London: Hogarth, 1957.

———(1918). From the history of an infantile neurosis. *Standard Edition* 17:7–22. London: Hogarth, 1955.

———(1919). Lines of advance in psychoanalytic therapy. *Standard Edition* 17:157–168. London: Hogarth, 1955.

———(1926a). Address to the society of B'nai B'rith. *Standard Edition* 20:271–274. London: Hogarth, 1959.

———(1926b). The question of lay analysis. *Standard Edition* 20:179–258. London: Hogarth, 1959.

———(1930). Civilization and its discontents. *Standard Edition* 21:59–145. London: Hogarth, 1961.

———(1933). New introductory lectures on psychoanalysis. *Standard Edition* 22:1–182. London: Hogarth, 1964.

———(1937). Analysis terminable and interminable. *Standard Edition* 23:211–253. London: Hogarth, 1964.

Gardner, R. W., Holzman, P. S., Klein, G. S., Linton, H. B., and Spence, D. P. (1959). Cognitive control: a study of individual consistencies in cognitive behavior. *Psychological Issues* 1(4):1–186.

Gill, M. (1954). Psychoanalysis and exploratory psychotherapy. *Journal of the American Psychoanalytic Association* 2:771–797.

Gittelson, M. (1952). The emotional position of the analyst in the psychoanalytical situation. *International Journal of Psycho-Analysis* 33:1–10.

Glover, E. (1931). The therapeutic effect of the inexact interpretation: a contribution to the theory of suggestion. *International Journal of Psycho-Analysis* 12(4):397–411.

————(1955). *The Technique of Psychoanalysis.* New York: International Universities Press.

Greenson, R. (1967). *The Technique and Practice of Psychoanalysis.* New York: International Universities Press.

Greenson, R., and Wexler, M. (1969). The nontransference relationship in the psychoanalytic situation. *International Journal of Psycho-Analysis* 50:27–39.

Grossart, A. B., ed. (1876). *The Prose Works of William Wordsworth,* 3 vols. London: Edward Moxon.

Guntrip, H. (1968). *Schizoid Phenomena, Object-Relations and the Self.* New York: International Universities Press.

Hartmann, H. (1951). Ego psychology and the problem of adaptation. In *Organization and Pathology of Thought,* ed. D. Rapaport. New York: Columbia University Press.

————(1964a). Comments on the psychoanalytic theory of the ego. In *Essays on Ego Psychology* by H. Hartmann. New York: International Universities Press.

————(1964b). On rational and irrational action. In *Essays on Ego Psychology* by H. Hartmann. New York: International Universities Press.

Holt, R. (1965). Ego autonomy re-evaluated. *International Journal of Psycho-Analysis* 46:151–167.

Holzman, P. S. (1974). The influence of theoretical models on the treatment of schizophrenia, reported by J. L. Gunderson. *Journal of the American Psychoanalytic Association* 22:182–199.

Holzman, P. S., and Gardner, R. W. (1960). Levelling and repression. *Journal of Abnormal Social Psychology* 59:151–155.

Horwitz, L. (1974). *Clinical Predictions in Psychotherapy.* New York: Jason Aronson.

Horwitz, L., and Appelbaum, S. A. (1966). A hierarchical ordering of assumptions about psychotherapy. *Psychotherapy* 3:7–80.

Housemann, A. E. (1933). *The Name and Nature of Poetry*. Cambridge: University Press.

Janov, A. (1970). *The Primal Scream*. New York: Putnam.

Jung, C. (1923). *Psychological Types or the Psychology of Individuation*. New York: Harcourt, Brace.

Klein, G. (1970). The ego in psychoanalysis: a concept in search of identity. *Psychoanalytic Review* 56:511-525.

Knight, R. (1953a). Borderline states. In *Psychoanalytic Psychiatry and Psychology*, ed. R. P. Knight and C. R. Friedman. New York: International Universities Press.

———(1953b). Evaluation of psychotherapeutic techniques. In *Psychoanalytic Psychiatry and Psychology*, ed. R. P. Knight and C. R. Friedman. New York: International Universities Press.

Kohut, H. (1959). Introspection, empathy and psychoanalysis. *Journal of the American Psychoanalytic Association* 7:459-482.

Kubie, L. (1958). *Neurotic Distortions of the Creative Process*. Lawrence: University of Kansas Press.

Kuiper, P. (1968). Indications and contraindications for psychoanalytic treatment. *International Journal of Psycho-Analysis* 49:261-264.

Kris, E. (1950). On preconscious mental processes. *Psychoanalytic Quarterly* 19:540-560.

———(1952). *Psychoanalytic Explorations in Art*. New York: International Universities Press.

———(1956). On some vicissitudes of insight in psychoanalysis. *International Journal of Psycho-Analysis* 37:445-455.

Langs, R. (1974). *The Technique of Psychoanalytic Psychotherapy*, vol. 2. New York: Jason Aronson.

Levitt, M., ed. (1959). *Readings in Psychoanalytic Psychology*. New York: Appleton-Century-Crofts.

Lewin, B. (1952). Phobic symptoms and dream interpretation. *Psychoanalytic Quarterly* 21:295-322.

Lewin, K. (1940). Formalization and progress in psychology. In *Field Theory in Social Science*, ed. D. Cartwright. New York: Harper, 1951.

Loewald, H. W. (1960). On the therapeutic action of psychoanalysis. *International Journal of Psycho-Analysis* 41:1-18.

Loewenstein, R. M. (1956). Some remarks on the role of speech in psychoanalytic technique. *International Journal of Psycho-Analysis* 37:460–467.

———(1967). Indications for psychoanalysis. *Kris Study Group of the New York Psychoanalytic Institute*, Monograph II:3–51. New York: International Universities Press.

Low, B. (1935). The psychological compensations of the analyst. *International Journal of Psycho-Analysis* 16:1–8.

Luborsky, L. (1953). Self-interpretation of the TAT as a clinical technique. *Journal of Projective Techniques* 17:217–223.

Mahler, M. S., Pine, F., and Bergman, A. (1975). *The Psychological Birth of the Human Infant*. New York: Basic Books.

Malan, D. H. (1963). *A Study of Brief Psychotherapy*. London: Tavistock.

Mann, J. (1973). *Time-Limited Psychotherapy*. Cambridge: University Press.

Marmor, J. (1964). Psychoanalytic therapy and theories of learning. In *Science and Psychoanalysis*, vol. 7, ed. J. Masserman. New York: Grune and Stratton.

McQuown, N. (1957). Linguistic transcription and specification of psychiatric interview materials. *Psychiatry* 20:79–86.

Menninger, K. (1937). The genius of the Jew in psychiatry. In *Medical Leaves*, vol. 1, ed. J. C. Beck. Chicago: Medical Leaves, Inc.

———(1958). *Theory of Psychoanalytic Technique*. 1st ed. New York: Basic Books.

Menninger, K., and Holzman, P. (1973). *Theory of Psychoanalytic Technique*. 2nd ed. New York: Basic Books.

Milner, M. (1952). Aspects of symbolism in the comprehension of the not-self. *International Journal of Psycho-Analysis* 33:181–195.

Mind Control Newsletter (1974). 5(3):5.

Moore, B. E., and Fine, B. D., eds. (1968). *A Glossary of Psychoanalytic Terms and Concepts*. New York: American Psychoanalytic Association.

Moses, R., and Kligler, D. S. (1966). A comparative analysis of the institutionalization of mental health values: the United States and Israel. *Israel Annals of Psychiatry* 4:148–160.

Namnum, A. (1968). The problem of analysability and the autonomous ego. *International Journal of Psycho-Analysis* 49:271–275.

Orens, M. H. (1955). Setting a termination date — an impetus to analysis. *Journal of the American Psychoanalytic Association* 3:651–665.

Parkinson, C. N. (1957). *Parkinson's Law*. Boston: Houghton Mifflin.

Perls, F. S. (1969a). *Ego, Hunger, and Aggression*. New York: Vintage Books.

———(1969b). *Gestalt Therapy Verbatim*. Moab: Real People Press.

Phillips, E. L., and Johnston, M. S. H. (1954). Theoretical and clinical aspects of short-term parent-child psychotherapy. *Psychiatry* 17:167–175.

Piaget, J. (1954). *The Construction of Reality in the Child*. New York: Basic Books.

Pittenger, R., Hockett, C. F., and Danehy, J. J. (1960). *The First Five Minutes*. Ithaca: Paul Martineau.

Popper, K. (1959). *The Logic of Scientific Discovery*. London: Hutchinson.

Ramzy, I. (1961). The range and spirit of psycho-analytic technique. *International Journal of Psycho-Analysis* 42:497–505.

Rangell, L. (1968). The psychoanalytic process. *International Journal of Psycho-Analysis* 49:19–26.

Rank, O. (1945). *Will Therapy and Truth and Reality*. New York: Knopf.

Rapaport, D. (1950). On the psychoanalytic theory of thinking. *International Journal of Psycho-Analysis* 31:1–10.

Rapaport, D., Gill, M. M., and Schafer, R. (1968). *Diagnostic Psychological Testing*, ed. R. Holt. New York: International Universities Press.

Reich, W. (1949). *Character Analysis*. 3rd ed. New York: Orgone Institute.

Reid, J., and Finesinger, J. (1952). The role of insight in psychotherapy. *American Journal of Psychiatry* 108:726–734.

Reik, T. (1933). New ways in psychoanalytic technique. *International Journal of Psycho-Analysis* 14:321–334.

———(1948). *Listening with the Third Ear*. New York: Farrar, Straus.

Richfield, J. (1954). An analysis of the concept of insight. *Psychoanalytic Quarterly* 23:390–408.

Rorschach, H. (1951). *Psychodiagnostics*. New York: Grune and Stratton.

Rosenzweig, S. (1936). Some implicit common factors in diverse methods of psychotherapy. *American Journal of Orthopsychiatry* 6:412–420.

Rousey, C., and Moriarity, A. (1965). *Diagnostic Implications of Speech Sounds.* Springfield: Chas. C Thomas.

Ruesch, J. (1961). *Therapeutic Communication.* New York: W. W. Norton and Co., Inc.

Schafer, R. (1959). Generative empathy in the treatment situation. *Psychoanalytic Quarterly* 28:342–373.

———(1968a). The mechanisms of defence. *International Journal of Psycho-Analysis* 49:49–62.

———(1968b). On the theoretical and technical conceptualizations of activity and passivity. *Psychoanalytic Quarterly* 37:173–198.

———(1970). The psychoanalytic vision of reality. *International Journal of Psycho-Analysis* 51:279–297.

———(1973a). Action: its place in psychoanalytic interpretation and theory. *Annual of Psychoanalysis* 1:169–196.

———(1973b). Concepts of self and identity and the experience of separation-individuation in adolescence. *Psychoanalytic Quarterly* 42:42–59.

———(1973c). The idea of resistance. *International Journal of Psycho-Analysis* 54:259–285.

———(1974). Talking to patients in psychotherapy. *Bulletin of the Menninger Clinic* 38:503–515.

———(1976). *A New Language for Psychoanalysis.* New Haven: Yale University Press.

Schlesinger, H. J. (1969). Promises, promises: making them set up a tension system. *Roche Report: Frontiers of Clinical Psychiatry* 6:5–6.

———(1977). The responsibility of the analyst for psychological change. Paper presented at the Topeka Psychoanalytic Society, Topeka, April.

———(1978). Development and regressive aspects of the making and breaking of promises. In *The Human Mind Revisited,* ed. S. Smith. New York: International Universities Press.

Shakespeare, W. *Hamlet,* act iii, sc. 2, lines 367–371.

Shannon, C., and Weaver, W. (1949). *The Mathematical Theory of Communication.* Urbana: University of Illinois Press.

Shapiro, A. (1971). Placebo effects in medicine, psychotherapy, and psychoanalysis. In *Handbook of Psychotherapy and Behavior Change*, ed. A. Bergin and S. Garfield. New York: John Wiley.

Shapiro, D. (1970). Motivation and action in psychoanalytic psychiatry. *Psychiatry* 33:329–342.

Sharpe, E. (1930). The technique of psychoanalysis. *International Journal of Psycho-Analysis* 11(3):251–277.

Sharpe, E. (1937). *Dream Analysis*. London: Hogarth Press, 1951.

Silva, J., and Miele, P. (1977). *The Silva Mind Control Method*. New York: Simon and Schuster.

Silverberg, W. (1955). Acting out versus insight: a problem in psychoanalytic technique. *Psychoanalytic Quarterly* 24:527–594.

Simonton, O. C., Matthews-Simonton, S., and Creighton, J. (1978). *Getting Well Again*. Los Angeles: J. P. Tarcher.

Stone, L. (1954). The widening scope of indications for psychoanalysis. *Journal of the American Psychoanalytic Association* 2:567–594.

——(1961). *The Psychoanalytic Situation: An Examination of Its Development and Essential Nature*. New York: International Universities Press.

——(1967). Indications for psychoanalysis. *Kris Study Group of the New York Psychoanalytic Institute*, Monograph II:3–51. New York: International Universities Press.

Strachey, J. (1934). The nature of the therapeutic action of psychoanalysis. *International Journal of Psycho-Analysis* 15:127–159.

Strupp, H. (1973). Toward a reformulation of the psychoanalytic influence. *International Journal of Psychiatry* 11:263–365.

Szigeti, J. (1963). Composer, performer, and audience. In *Conflict and Creativity*. New York: McGraw-Hill.

Tarachow, S. (1965). Ambiguity and human imperfection. *Journal of the American Psychoanalytic Association* 13:85–101.

Thass-Thienemann, T. (1963). Psychotherapy and linguistics. *Topical Problems of Psychotherapy* 4:37–45.

Toman, W. (1976). *Family Constellation*. New York: Springer-Verlag.

Tompkins, C. (1965). Not seen and/or less seen. *New Yorker*, 40(15) February 6, pp. 37–93.

Waldhorn, H. (1960). Assessment of analysability: technical and theoretical observations. *Psychoanalytic Quarterly* 29:478–506.

————(1967). Indications for psychoanalysis. *Kris Study Group of the New York Psychoanalytic Institute*, Monograph II:3–51. New York: International Universities Press.

Wallerstein, R. S., and Robbins, L. (1956). The psychotherapy research project of the Menninger foundation. *Bulletin of the Menninger Clinic* 20:221–278.

Werner, H. (1948). *Comparative Psychology of Mental Development*. Chicago: Follett Pub. Co.

Wheelis, A. B. (1950). The place of action in personality change. *Psychiatry* 13:135–158.

————(1956). Will and psychoanalysis. *Journal of the American Psychoanalytic Association* 4:285–303.

————(1973). *How People Change*. New York: Harper and Row, Pub.

White, R. W. (1963). Ego and reality in psychoanalytic theory. *Psychological Issues* 3(3):1–210.

Winnicott, D. (1965). *The Maturational Processes and the Facilitating Environment: Studies in the Theory of Emotional Development*. New York: International Universities Press.

Wisdom, J. (1975). A critical assessment of the future of psychoanalysis: a view from the outside. *Journal of the American Psychoanalytic Association* 23:587–602.

Yontef, G. M. (1969). Theory of Gestalt therapy. In *The Handbook of Gestalt Therapy*, eds. C. Hatcher and P. Himelstein. New York: Jason Aronson, 1976.

————(1971). *A Review of the Practice of Gestalt Therapy*. Los Angeles: Trident, California State College.

Index